BALLOTS TO BENEFITS

TO

BENEFITS

BALL⊗TS TO BENEFITS

THE IMPACT OF PRE-ELECTION SOCIAL SCHEMES IN INDIA

PRAVEEN RAO

Inkfeathers Publishing
www.inkfeathers.com

Mayank Das, CEO, Audio Bridge India

"This publication surely provides a great insight about the importance and effects of elections and public schemes which many of us are not aware of. The author has done a wonderful job by bringing his well-researched content in the form of book which is going to help millions of people in understanding the importance of their votes, also the impact of elections and public schemes on General Public."

Naveen Kumar, IAS, Government of Uttar Pradesh

"Drawing on a distinguished career as a public sector advisor, the author masterfully presented an incisive and enlightening analysis about social schemes. This book stands as a testament to both the author's expertise and the critical importance of the subject matter. A must-read for anyone interested in the intersection of politics, policy, and public welfare."

Ajitabh Sharma, IAS, Government of Rajasthan

"In my interactions with Praveen Rao, his unwavering dedication to good governance and tireless efforts in spotlighting social issues have left a deep impression. With enthusiasm, I eagerly anticipate the positive change he'll bring."

Amit Mali, Public Sector Advisor, Deloitte India

"This book is an apt coverage of economics and politics of the social schemes. It offers a deep dive into the context, significance, political dynamics, and economic consequences of social schemes. It is a must-read for anyone interested in understanding the role of social welfare in Indian politics and economics. Praveen has great experience in working with various governments and bureaucrats and it has come out befittingly in his writing with his astute analytical skills."

Saumya Mehta, Infrastructure support Specialist, KPMG India

"Praveen Rao's expertise in this field is clearly demonstrated, making the book a reliable and informative resource for anyone interested in understanding the outcomes of social welfare initiatives in India. The book has a data-driven approach contribute to its credibility and relevance. Wishing him all the best!"

**Rohit Saxena, Investment Accounting Expert,
Associate Director, SS&C Technologies**

"Author has not tried to cut corners by any means. His impressive work on ground in related matters and with detailed research, he has done the needed justification and able to conclude the vastness of the subject into well-articulated points. I wish him all the best on his first book."

Himanshu Gupta, Senior Vice President, Bank of America

"This publication is an excellent representation of current state and need of future. Praveen has an exceptional track record in strategic consulting, particularly within government sectors. His expertise has been pivotal in redefining development plans and delivering outstanding results in growth strategy and performance improvement."

**Sudheer Goutam, Founder, CEO & Editor-In-Chief,
Indiglobal Media Network**

"It's bold, credible, and powered with insightful data. Praveen Rao's rich experience in the public domain reflects in this book – 'Ballots to Benefits.' This is one book for those who are looking for a comprehensive understanding and analysis of political agendas for the electoral outcomes, impact, socio-economic developments, and its financial implications."

To all the hidden heroes and citizens of this country

who directly or indirectly contribute towards a

Good Governance & Nation building.

Contents

Preface

In the democratic fabric of our society, elections are moments of profound significance. They are the bedrock of our collective voice, allowing us to shape the course of our nation's future. As the electorate, we can choose leaders representing our interests, champion our causes, and pave the way for a better tomorrow.

However, the electoral process is not confined solely to casting ballots. It is a complex tapestry of promises, policies, and social schemes that shape the discourse leading up to election day. In this book, we delve into the intricate world of social plans before elections, examining the intersection of politics, policymaking, and the aspirations of our society.

Social schemes, with their potential to uplift and transform lives, often take center stage during election campaigns. They represent the mechanisms through which political parties and candidates communicate their vision and commitment to addressing the pressing obligations of the people. These schemes promise many benefits, from economic empowerment to social welfare, healthcare, education, and beyond.

The purpose of this book is not to advocate for or critique any political ideology or party. Instead, it serves as a comprehensive exploration of the phenomenon of social schemes in the context of elections, shedding light on the intricate dynamics at play. We seek to uncover these schemes' underlying motivations, strategies, and impacts, aiming to give readers a deeper understanding of their significance and implications.

Throughout the following chapters, we embark on a journey traversing social schemes' intricacies before elections. We examine the historical context, analyzing the evolution of these schemes over time and their influence on electoral outcomes. We delve into the policy frameworks that underpin their design, assessing their efficacy, feasibility, and potential for long-term societal impact.

Moreover, we explore the ethical dimensions of social schemes before elections, considering the fine line between genuine social welfare and mere political posturing. We reflect on the challenges in implementing these schemes, the potential for corruption or exploitation, and the imperative of transparency in ensuring their success.

"Ballots to Benefits" does not claim to have all the answers, but it does aim to ask the right questions.

We hope this book will serve as a valuable resource by shedding light on the complexities and nuances of this sensation, and we line up to foster a more informed electorate empowered to evaluate the promises made during election campaigns critically.

As we embark on this exploration, let us remember our immense power as citizens. Our responsibility lies not only in casting our votes but also in holding our elected representatives accountable for the assurances they made. By understanding the dynamics of social schemes before elections, we can contribute to creating a more transparent, equitable, and comprehensive democratic process.

As an author, I invite you to approach "Ballots to Benefits" with an open mind. Whether you are a student, a policymaker, an academic, or an engaged citizen, this book aims to provoke thought, stimulate debate, and offer insights into the nexus between social welfare and political strategy.

I want to express my gratitude to my friends, family, and mentors who have supported me throughout the writing process. Their invaluable feedback, constructive criticism, and unwavering encouragement have brought this work to fruition.

Thank you for embarking on this intellectual journey with me. I trust that you will find "Ballots to Benefits" as intriguing to read as it was for me to research and write.

Praveen Rao

Chapter One

Welfarism in India

Welfarism is a political and socio-economic philosophy that emphasizes the well-being and welfare of individuals within a society. In India, welfarism has played a significant role in shaping social policies and programs aimed at uplifting the disadvantaged sections of society.

India, a country rich in history and culture, has also been a long-standing model for welfarism. With a population of over 1.3 billion, the responsibility to ensure the welfare of its citizens is no small task. As the world's largest democracy, India has struggled with the complexities and challenges of providing basic amenities and social services to an incredibly diverse populace, both culturally and economically.

By analyzing the historical context, various initiatives, and the impact of welfarism in India, we can better understand the country's commitment to social justice.

Welfare in India can be traced back to Vedic times, when the concept of "Dharma" emphasized social responsibilities, including the interest of one's fellow citizens. Various rulers and dynasties incorporated welfare into their governance structures long before the modern nation-state was established.

For instance, the Mauryan Empire, one of the earliest empires in the Indian subcontinent, emphasized welfare as an essential part of governance. Ancient texts such as Chanakya's Arthashastra explains an elaborate administrative system that included welfare provisions like food storage for times of famine, public healthcare, and state-sponsored education.

The Gupta period, often termed the 'Golden Age' of India, saw the establishment of educational institutions like Nalanda and medical facilities, demonstrating an early form of state responsibility towards welfare.

Even during the Medieval period, rulers like Akbar and Sher Shah Suri implemented systems that facilitated public welfare, such as road networks and rest houses for traveler's, which were strategic assets and welfare measures.

The Colonial Period: A Shift in Paradigms

The advent of colonial rule by the British in the 18th century brought about a significant shift in governance and welfare. While the British did establish some welfare measures like famine relief, their primary focus was resource extraction and control, which often clashed with the welfare needs of the local population. Many social policies implemented during this period were not aimed at holistic welfare but were often band-aid solutions to complex problems.

The adverse effects of colonial rule—like social and economic inequality—left a lasting impact on the country, presenting the newly independent India with considerable challenges for ensuring public welfare.

Post-Independence: Ideals and Realities

After gaining independence in 1947, India adopted a democratic form of governance and a constitution emphasizing social justice. Welfare was integral to the new nation's ambitions, and a series of Five-Year Plans were implemented to provide a structured approach to economic and social development. Inspired by the Soviet model, these plans aimed to improve agricultural productivity, industrial output, social welfare, education, healthcare, and rural development.

Initially, the focus was on economic development and nation-building. However, as it became evident that economic growth was not trickling down to the disadvantaged sections of society, there was a shift towards direct welfare interventions.

Challenges: Implementing Welfarism in a Complex Landscape

Implementing welfare policies in India is a Herculean task due to its diversity, population size, and socio-economic disparities. The country's federal structure adds another layer of complexity, as welfare is often a subject that falls under the joint purview of the central and state governments.

Let's understand this in detail.

One of the most significant challenges is targeting welfare benefits effectively. There is a high risk of exclusion errors, where deserving beneficiaries are left out, and inclusion errors, where undeserving individuals are included.

Another debate is whether to focus on the breadth or the depth of welfare programs. Should policies aim for broader coverage, often at the expense of the quality of services, or should they aim for a more profound impact, even if it means fewer beneficiaries?

Bureaucratic delays, corruption, and lack of transparency have often created significant obstacles in implementing welfare policies effectively. Welfare schemes may sometimes be used as political tools rather than mechanisms for social good. This politicization can affect the efficiency and effectiveness of these programs.

Welfare policies often stir ideological debates. For some, welfarism is seen as an essential obligation of the state towards its citizens, especially those who are disadvantaged. Others argue that too much dependence on welfare can lead to economic inefficiencies and stifle individual initiative.

Moreover, the concept of welfare is often intertwined with identity politics in India, as caste, religion, and region can sometimes determine access to welfare benefits. This can lead to divisive politics and social tensions, further complicating the welfare landscape.

Future Directions: Evolving Frameworks

While India has yet to find a perfect formula for welfarism, several emerging trends offer hope. Decentralization of welfare administration to local levels provides the promise of more targeted and effective delivery. Non-governmental organizations (NGOs) and civil society have also increasingly contributed to shaping and implementing welfare policies.

Moreover, academic and policy discourse is leaning towards more evidence-based approaches, utilizing data and empirical studies to design and implement welfare schemes. While challenges remain, these developments indicate India's increasingly sophisticated approach to welfare.

India's journey in welfarism has been long and complex, shaped by its rich history and faced with contemporary challenges. The country's approach to welfare is a layered narrative, often juggling various ideological, administrative, and socio-economic factors. As India continues its journey towards becoming a more equitable society, the lessons from its history and its present challenges will be crucial in shaping a more nuanced and compelling welfare system for its diverse and populous nation.

Recently, India has implemented several social schemes to address poverty, inequality, and social exclusion. These initiatives aim to help with a safety net for the discriminated sections of society and uplift them from poverty and deprivation.

The social schemes implemented in India reflect the underlying principles of welfarism. These programs are designed to ensure that the assistance reaches the weaker sections of society and alleviates their socio-economic hardships.

India has been instrumental in shaping social policies and programs to improve the well-being and welfare of the country's citizens. Through initiatives like MGNREGA, NFSA, PMJDY, PMUY, AB-PMJAY, and many more, India has made significant strides in poverty alleviation, social inclusion, human development, and empowerment.

India's journey in the realm of welfarism has been a long and complex one. The country's approach to welfare is a layered narrative, often juggling various ideological, administrative, and socio-economic factors.

Welfarism in India is deeply rooted in the country's history, with each era contributing to its evolution and refinement. While the ancient and medieval periods saw welfare as an extension of rulers' duties and benevolence, the modern era, especially post-independence, has seen it transform into a right, institutionalized through constitutional and policy frameworks.

As India continues to become a more equitable society, the lessons from its history and its present challenges will be crucial in shaping a more nuanced and compelling welfare system for its diverse and populous nation.

However, challenges remain in ensuring constructive implementation, enhancing administrative capacity, and sustaining the financial viability of these social schemes.

Despite these concerns, welfarism remains an important goal for India. The government has a responsibility to ensure that all citizens have the opportunity to live a decent life.

Chapter Two

Understanding Pre-Election Social Schemes: Context & Significance

India is a country with diverse income stagnation challenges and a large population. Elections, which occur periodically at various levels, provide an opportunity for political parties to present their vision for addressing challenges in the society.

In the vibrant democracy of India, the period leading up to elections witnesses a surge in the announcement of social schemes by political parties. These schemes are strategically designed to address social issues and cater to demographics to influence public opinion and gain electoral support.

The announcement of social schemes before elections serves as a powerful tool to engage with the electorate and showcase the party's commitment to social welfare.

Pre-election social schemes play a crucial role in the Indian political landscape. They are instrumental in addressing social issues and meeting the citizen's requirements and serve as potent tools for political messaging and gaining electoral support. While the significance of these schemes lies in their ability to sway public opinion, their impact can extend beyond elections, leading to practical long-term payoffs for society.

India is known for its social welfare schemes that aim to elevate the economically weaker elements of society. These schemes have been a crucial part of the electoral strategies of political parties in India, especially in the run-up to the elections. The pre-election social projects in India have become a matter of debate, with some arguing that they are necessary to uplift people experiencing poverty. In contrast, others disagree that they are just an attraction to gain votes.

Authorities and political parties realized that voters can swayed by promises of free food, subsidized healthcare, and other social schemes. They are less interested in long-term plans for the country and more interested in getting what they can right now.

This is why people in power or wish to be in power focus on short-term populist measures rather than on policies that will benefit the country in the long run. They know that they will be re-elected if they can give the voters what they want.

But the truth is that the majority of Indian voters are more interested in their welfare than in the interest of the country. And this is why social schemes are so effective in swaying their votes.

Of course, this is not to say that all Indian voters are short-sighted. Many are genuinely concerned about the future of the country and who vote for the candidates who they believe will best represent their interests.

Some of the questions are the need of the hour.

- What are the long-term consequences of this trend?
- Are we creating a generation of voters who are only interested in short-term gains and are not willing to think about the country's future?
- Why Indian Voters Are Attracted Towards Social Schemes ?

Let's understand this through some of the most common reasons, including:

- Poverty: Many Indians live below the poverty line. Social schemes provide them with a much-needed source of income and support.

- Unemployment: Social schemes can help create jobs and provide people with a livelihood.
- Inequality: Social schemes can help reduce inequality and give everyone a fair chance in life.
- Illiteracy: Social schemes can improve literacy rates and give people the skills they need to succeed in life.
- Healthcare: Social schemes can help people access healthcare and improve their quality of life.

There are a few reasons why many Indian voters see only short-term benefits from social schemes.

Some of the most common causes include:

- Lack of awareness: They may need to understand the long-term benefits of social schemes and be more interested in the immediate benefits, such as free food or money.
- Poverty: Poverty can make people desperate. They may be more willing to vote for politicians who promise them immediate benefits, even if those benefits are not sustainable in the long run.
- Misinformation: Politicians and other vested interests often spread misinformation about social schemes. They may claim that the systems are more beneficial than they are, or they may hide the long-term costs of the schemes.
- Culture: In India, there is a strong emphasis on immediate gratification. People may be more willing to take short-term gains, even if they know they must pay for them in the long run.

Social schemes have a significant impact on Indian politics. They can help to determine who gets elected, and they can also shape the policies that the government implements.

In recent years, there has been a trend towards populist legislators who promise to provide more social schemes. These lawmakers often appeal to the poor and the marginalized, and they can succeed in elections.

However, social schemes can also have a negative impact on Indian politics. They can lead to corruption, as politicians may use them to enrich themselves or their supporters. They can also be unsustainable and strain the government's finances. Indian voters who get attracted by seeing short-term benefits will always see troubles in the future.

Let's now move further.

Social schemes before elections can be a significant factor in swaying voters' opinions. This is because these schemes often equip instant well-being voters, such as cash transfers, food rations, or access to healthcare. This can make voters more likely to vote for the party offering these benefits.

In addition, social schemes can be used to target multiple batches of voters. For example, a party might offer a system that provides financial assistance to farmers to win their votes. This type of targeting can be highly constructive in winning elections.

However, it is essential to note that social schemes can also be seen as a form of vote buying. This is because they are often offered or highlighted when the election is close, and voters are most likely to be swayed by short-term benefits.

If voters believe they are being bribed, they may be less likely to keep up the party offering the scheme in the long run. Overall, the significance of social schemes before elections depends on several factors, including the type of scheme, target group, and project timing. However, there is no doubt that these schemes can be a powerful tool for winning elections.

As election campaigns gain momentum, political parties often resort to various strategies to gain voters' trust. One such strategy that has gained prominence is the imposition of pre-election social schemes.

These schemes are designed to target various parts of society and look to address their socioeconomic needs. Social schemes, also known as social welfare programs or safety nets, are crucial in stimulating social equity and addressing societal inequality. Governments worldwide implement these programs to assure affirmation to vulnerable individuals and groups.

Pre-election social schemes have been an integral part of India's growth strategy, aimed at reducing poverty, improving health outcomes, and providing financial inclusion to critical chapters of society. These schemes have successfully achieved their goals but have also faced significant challenges in their results.

Political parties play a crucial role in shaping the socioeconomic landscape of a nation. One significant aspect of their agenda is the commitment to various social schemes to address the people's wishes and foster inclusive development. These social schemes hold immense significance as they point to edifying empowered sections, alleviating poverty, shoring up essential services, and empowering communities.

These schemes reflect political parties' commitment to governance, welfare, and inclusive development. By implementing these schemes, parties contribute to the nation's overall well-being, fostering social stability, economic growth, and a more integrative society.

Political parties must ensure practical monitoring and evaluation of these schemes to maximize their impact and ensure that they reach the intended beneficiaries. Only through sustained commitment and accountability can these social schemes create lasting constructive change in the lives of the people they focus on serving.

Contextually, a country like India, with many socioeconomic imbalances Like poverty, unemployment, healthcare, and education, remain critical areas that need attention.

By recognizing these challenges, political parties use pre-election social schemes to connect with the masses and win their support. These schemes typically provide welfare measures, subsidies, and targeted aid to multiple groups or communities.

Accepting such schemes coincides with the electoral cycle, with parties hoping to sway public sentiment in their favor. Social welfare schemes have become an integral part of the Indian political landscape, especially in the run-up to the necessity for uplifting people experiencing poverty; others argue that they are a form of attraction for the voters. The effectiveness and feasibility of these schemes continue to be a matter of debate.

In authoritarian regimes like China, social schemes serve to monitor and control the population. For instance, the Social Credit System in China leverages data and surveillance to evaluate citizens' behavior and allocate rewards or penalties accordingly. While this system extends beyond traditional social welfare programs, it demonstrates how social schemes can be utilized to exercise control over individuals and shape societal behavior.

These schemes also serve as a tool for political parties to build a direct rapport with the electorate. By implementing social welfare programs, parties can establish themselves as champions of the underprivileged and gain their trust and support.

Providing subsidies, healthcare facilities, education grants, and other perquisites through pre-election schemes creates a perception that the ruling party is committed to addressing the necessity of the people, thereby increasing its chances of electoral success.

However, the execution of pre-election social schemes also raises concerns about their timing and sustainability. Critics attest that these schemes are often launched hastily before elections, raising doubts about their long-term viability and impact.

Some political parties have been accused of using these schemes as mere electoral sops rather than genuine efforts to bring about meaningful change. Additionally, The administration must carefully evaluate such schemes' financial burden and potential impact on economic profile to ensure fiscal prudence.

As per a coverage done by The Times of India , "In a marathon meeting of Prime Minister of India with senior bureaucrats, a few officials raised concern over populist schemes announced by several states, claiming they are economically unsustainable and could take them down the same path as Sri Lanka."

Social schemes can enhance legitimacy, promote social stability, and contribute to economic growth. However, they can also be used as mechanisms for social control and face troubles in achieving results. It is fair to critically assess the impact of social schemes in specific contexts, considering the broader political landscape and the population's well-being.

Social schemes contribute by reducing inequality and addressing grievances. In countries across Asia, including China, where social inequalities have been a concern, the government has implemented various schemes to address poverty and improve social conditions. These efforts have helped maintain stability and prevent social unrest by addressing the issues of vulnerable populations and reducing income disparities.

Furthermore, pre-election social schemes can lead to the politicization of welfare programs, where aid may be selectively distributed based on political affiliations. This practice undermines the principles of balanced leadership and can deepen societal divisions. Establishing independent oversight mechanisms to ensure these schemes' fair and transparent performance is essential to mitigate this risk.

Let us understand the strategies for addressing the socioeconomic challenges of elections worldwide & critical aspects highlighting the significance of these schemes.

Addressing Socioeconomic Challenges

Elections are crucial milestones in democratic societies, allowing citizens to choose their leaders and shape the future of their nations. However, elections also present socioeconomic challenges that need to be addressed. These challenges include increased political polarization, resource allocation, disruptions to economic activities, and potential social unrest.

Let us understand the strategies for addressing the socioeconomic challenges of elections worldwide.

India faces numerous socioeconomic challenges like poverty, unemployment, healthcare deficiencies, and educational disparities. Pre-election schemes are designed to target these challenges and develop welfare measures and subsidies for certain sections of society. By doing so, these schemes aim to alleviate poverty, improve access to essential services, and bridge socioeconomic gaps.

Empowering Marginalized Sections

Pre-election schemes often empower weaker sections of society, including farmers, women, scheduled castes and tribes, and economically troubled units. Through initiatives like farm loan waivers, financial inclusion programs, skill-forming schemes, and reservation policies, these schemes wish to uplift the disadvantaged and cater to them with opportunities for socioeconomic growth.

In Asian countries like China, where groups may face challenges in accessing political representation and resources, it becomes imperative to take proactive measures to empower these sections.

Before the elections in China, many efforts were made to enhance their political participation, and it was achieved through various means, such as advocating voter registration campaigns targeted at weaker communities, creating awareness about their voting rights, and providing voter education programs. Encouraging the formation of community-based organizations and grassroots movements has also empowered fragile batches to voice their concerns and advocate for their rights.

Direct Engagement with the Electorate

Implementing pre-election schemes allows political parties to directly engage with the electorate and establish a connection based on welfare and development. By supporting tangible aid and addressing the prompt requirement of the people, parties can build trust and gain support, enhancing their chances of electoral success.

Direct engagement with the electorate is vital for productive democratic governance. Political leaders can enhance representation, accountability, and trust by involving citizens directly. It facilitates unrestricted decision-making, ensuring that diverse voices are heard, and mobilizes grassroots activities for active citizenship. Embracing direct engagement allows leaders to forge stronger connections with their constituents, fostering a sense of ownership and participation in the political process.

Additionally, direct engagement can help bridge the gap between many politicians and the public. By meeting face-to-face or engaging through digital platforms, leaders humanize themselves and become more accessible. This accessibility and open communication increase public confidence in the political process and nurture a sense of ownership and investment in democratic institutions.

As democratic societies continue to evolve, the importance of direct engagement should be recognized and nurtured, empowering citizens, and shaping policies that reflect their aspirations and needs.

Enhancing Voter Turnout

Pre-election schemes can also influence voter turnout. When people perceive that a particular political party or government has implemented welfare schemes that benefit them, they are more likely to participate in the electoral process and exercise their voting rights. This increased voter turnout strengthens the democratic fabric of the nation.

Voter turnout, the percentage of eligible voters who cast their ballots in an election, is a crucial factor in democratic processes. A high voter turnout signifies an engaged and active citizenry, resulting in more representative and legitimate outcomes.

By encouraging broader participation in the electoral process, societies can ensure that the voices of all citizens are heard and that elected representatives openly reflect the will of the people they serve. Social schemes committed before elections are a worthwhile tool for attracting voter support. Parties strategically design these schemes to appeal to set voter demographics and win their loyalty.

For example, schemes targeting farmers may include loan waivers or agricultural subsidies. In contrast, techniques aimed at women may focus on financial inclusion or empowerment.

By offering palpable rewards and directly addressing the concerns of different voter groups, parties seek to secure their stand at the ballot box. When citizens perceive that a particular party or government has implemented welfare schemes that benefit them, they are more likely to participate in the electoral process and exercise their voting rights.

The promise of improved living conditions and access to essential services motivates voters to engage in the electoral process. Higher voter turnout strengthens the democratic fabric of the nation and ensures a more extensive representation of citizens' voices.

Accountability and Public Scrutiny

The execution of pre-election schemes puts political parties and governments under public scrutiny. It acts as a deterrent against abuse and fraud within social schemes. When these programs are subject to public scrutiny, it becomes more challenging for individuals or groups to exploit the system for personal gain. The fear of exposure and public backlash acts as a preventive measure, ensuring that resources are channeled appropriately to those in need.

It also encourages citizen engagement and participation in formulating and evaluating social schemes. When the public has access to information and can dispense input, they feel a sense of ownership over these programs.

This involvement fosters a more mature decision-making process, allowing the public to shape policies that directly affect their lives and ensuring that social schemes are responsive to the diversified profile of the population.

Citizens closely observe the delivery of promised assistance and hold political representatives accountable for their affirmation. This accountability fosters a sense of responsibility among elected officials and encourages them to fulfill their promises, ensuring better governance.

Addressing Immediate Needs

Pre-election social schemes are designed to address the immediate requirements of the people, particularly in areas where socioeconomic challenges persist. By focusing on these pressing issues, parties aspire to alleviate citizens' hardships and furnish rapid relief.

These schemes often target poorer sections of society, including farmers, women, economically disadvantaged groups, and minorities. By addressing their needs, parties demonstrate empathy and seek to win their trust in the upcoming elections.

Enhancing Political Legitimacy

Political legitimacy is essential for the functioning of democratic systems. It ensures that governments have the authority and public reinforcement duty to govern effectively. In India and the United States, political legitimacy was crucial in maintaining trust in the democratic process and advocating complete governance.

Implementing pre-election social schemes enhances the political legitimacy of parties. By committing to these schemes, parties signal their intent to govern responsibly and prioritize the welfare of the people.

Successfully running these schemes improves the party's credibility and enhances its image as a responsible political entity. This, in turn, helps build trust and confidence among the electorate, leading to a more robust mandate and legitimacy for the party.

Poverty Alleviation

Poverty alleviation requires a comprehensive and multifaceted approach combining social welfare programs, employment initiatives, education and skills development, and targeted interventions.

Likewise, European nations have made significant strides in reducing poverty rates and encouraging social inclusion. Continuous evaluation and adjustment of these strategies based on evolving societal requirements are crucial. Collaboration between governments, civil society organizations, and international institutions is vital to share best practices and ensure the result-oriented output of poverty alleviation measures.

By prioritizing poverty eradication, European countries have created a more fair and prosperous future for all their citizens. Political and social schemes play a crucial role in poverty alleviation by providing targeted assistance to weaker sections of society. These schemes are planned to improve access to education, healthcare, housing, and livelihood opportunities, lifting people out of poverty and reducing income inequalities.

Inclusive Development

Political and social schemes publicize inclusive development by addressing the ailing circles such as scheduled castes, tribes, and minorities. These schemes aim to empower these groups and bridge the socioeconomic divide by providing targeted opportunities.

Access to Education and Skill Development

Social schemes in India focus on improving access to quality education and skill enhancement programs. These schemes strive to equip individuals with the necessary tools to succeed in the job market and improve their socioeconomic status by arranging scholarships, free education, vocational training, and skill enhancement initiatives.

Public Health Initiatives

Political and social schemes prioritize healthcare and public health initiatives to ensure accessible and affordable healthcare for all citizens. These schemes include health insurance programs, immunization drives, maternal and child health programs, and establishing healthcare infrastructure in remote areas.

Women's Empowerment

Political and social schemes in India specifically focus on women's empowerment. These schemes are lined up to address gender inequalities by supporting financial assistance, skill development, and taking a stand for women entrepreneurs.

Schemes such as *Beti Bachao Beti Padhao* (Save the Girl Child, Educate the Girl Child) focus on assisting the rights and well-being of girls.

Rural Development

Social schemes in India prioritize uplifting rural communities and addressing agricultural challenges. Projects such as MGNREGA (Mahatma Gandhi National Rural Employment Guarantee Act) create employment opportunities and enhance rural infrastructure.

Financial Inclusion

Political and social schemes emphasize financial inclusion by furnishing banking services, subsidies, and direct benefit transfers to the incapacitated part of society. These schemes aim to bring the unbanked population into the formal financial system and reduce leakages and corruption in the distribution of benefits.

Environmental Conservation

With growing environmental concerns, political and social schemes increasingly focus on environmental conservation and maintainable development. Schemes like Swachh Bharat Abhiyan (Clean India Mission) and Pradhan Mantri Ujjwala Yojana (Clean Cooking Fuel Scheme) endorse cleanliness, sanitation, and access to clean energy, contributing to a healthier environment.

Social Harmony and Inclusion

Political and social schemes are positioned to foster social harmony and inclusion by providing equal opportunities to all segments of society. By stimulating affirmative action, reservation policies, and minority welfare schemes, these initiatives strive to reduce social discrimination and ensure equal participation.

Nation-Building

Political and social schemes support nation-building by addressing social issues, reducing disparities, and encouraging the overall well-being of citizens. These schemes create a sense of collective responsibility, citizenship, and belonging, fostering national unity and progress.

Political and social schemes in India have immense significance in addressing poverty, upgrading total development, giving access to education and healthcare, empowering women, supporting rural communities, elevating financial inclusion, fostering environmental conservation, ensuring social harmony, and contributing to nation-building.

These schemes are instrumental in improving citizens' quality of life and advancing the country's growth.

The significance of pre-election social schemes lies in their potential to bring about tactile advantages to the people and influence electoral outcomes. These schemes allow parties to engage with the electorate directly, demonstrating their concern for the well-being of the people and their commitment to addressing their needs.

By announcing and implementing these schemes, parties create a platform for interaction, which helps build trust and establish a connection with voters. This engagement enhances the party's image and reputation, ultimately shaping voter perception and influencing their decision at the ballot box.

Social schemes have the capacity to deliver benefits that positively impact the lives of millions. By targeting critical areas such as education, healthcare, rural development, and women empowerment, these schemes aim to bridge socioeconomic gaps and promote universal growth.

Education-focused schemes deliver access to quality education, scholarships, and vocational training, equipping individuals with the skills necessary for better employment opportunities and improved socioeconomic status.

The resulting encouragement creates a ripple effect, benefiting entire communities and contributing to economic development.

Social schemes also play a pivotal role in shaping electoral results by connecting with voters and gaining their support. Political parties strategically announce comprehensive and integrative social schemes to demonstrate their commitment to addressing societal concerns and improving citizens' lives.

The concrete value derived from these schemes creates a positive perception among voters, influencing their electoral decisions.

Social schemes targeted at multiple demographics, such as farmers, women, youth, or demoralized communities, mobilize and consolidate electoral bases. Political parties can earn their trust and loyalty by addressing these groups' unique obligations and aspirations. Successful carrying out of these schemes showcases a party's dedication to the whole development, significantly influencing the electorate's perception of its governance capabilities.

Social schemes provide an opportunity for political accountability. Voters evaluate the performance and impact of these schemes when making electoral choices. Parties that successfully implement social projects and deliver substantial perks will likely gain public trust and support.

Conversely, parties that fail to fulfill their promises or implement schemes ineffectively may face electoral backlash, highlighting the power of social systems to shape electoral outcomes.

Furthermore, pre-election social schemes shape the electoral narrative by focusing attention on specific issues and policy agendas. Parties strategically select plans that resonate with the electorate, ensuring that their promises align with the concerns and priorities of the people.

By emphasizing these schemes, parties shape the public discourse and set the agenda for electoral debates.

Therefore, these schemes' significance extends beyond immediate sake and welfare provisions. They invest in the broader democratic process by influencing the conversation around lead issues and shaping the direction of policy debates. Pre-election social schemes are crucial for political parties to attract voters and supply necessities to society's poor and susceptible sections.

The schemes have successfully reduced poverty, improved health outcomes, and provided financial inclusion. However, several challenges are associated with their implementation, such as corruption, lack of awareness, and inadequate infrastructure.

Sustained efforts are needed from the government, civil society, and other stakeholders to ensure the discharge of pre-election social schemes. Only then can the schemes achieve their intended objectives and brace society's poor and susceptible sections.

Pre-election social schemes are also strategically designed to target voter demographics in India. Parties identify key constituencies, such as farmers, women, youth, and peripheral edge people, and tailor their schemes to address their dedicated needs and aspirations.

For instance, agricultural loan waivers, crop insurance, and irrigation schemes are often aimed at attracting farmer votes, while initiatives boosting women's empowerment and financial inclusion cater to the interests of women voters. By targeting various demographics, parties plan to secure the loyalty of crucial voter segments.

Introducing pre-election social schemes also serves as a tool for electoral mobilization and increasing voter turnout. By announcing plans that benefit the electorate, parties seek to motivate voters to participate actively in the electoral process.

Pre-election social schemes play a significant role in shaping the image and popularity of political parties. Parties use these schemes to project themselves as pro-poor, welfare-oriented entities committed to addressing the undermined & underprivileged portion of society.

Successfully carrying through these schemes enhances the credibility and perception of parties as responsible political entities, which can positively influence their popularity and electoral prospects. Conversely, failure to deliver on promised schemes can lead to a loss of trust and voter disillusionment.

Vote bank politics is another critical political dynamic associated with pre-election social schemes in India. Parties often focus on social, religious, or caste-based vote banks and design schemes to cater to their interests.

This approach aims to consolidate pacts from various communities by addressing their socioeconomic concerns. By targeting certain vote banks, parties act to maximize electoral gains by securing the loyalty of influential and numerically significant voter groups. India's political landscape is highly diverse, with regional and state dynamics significantly formulating pre-election social schemes.

Parties tailor their schemes to cater to different regions and states' unique needs and aspirations. For instance, in rural states, parties may prioritize agricultural subsidies and irrigation tasks. In contrast, infrastructural growth and employment generation schemes may take precedence in urban centers.

Recognizing the regional and state dynamics is crucial for parties to resonate with the local population and gain electoral traction. Pre-election social schemes also subject political parties to scrutiny and accountability. Opposition parties and civil society organizations closely monitor the necessity or impact of these schemes.

Any perceived shortcomings or failures in delivering the promised blessing can lead to criticism and pessimistic public perception. The political dynamics surrounding pre-election social schemes necessitate parties to be accountable and responsive to the people's concerns.

Grasping the political dynamics underpinning these pre-election social schemes is essential to thoroughly learn their influence on India's electoral landscape and broader socio-political environment. Pre-election social schemes are inherently tied to electoral politics. Political parties strategically announce and implement these schemes to influence voter behavior and gain electoral support.

Parties always work towards creating a hopeful understanding among voters by showcasing their commitment to social welfare and addressing the essentials of the electorate. It also targets vibrant demographic groups that hold significant electoral influence. Parties identify multiple voter segments, such as farmers, youth, women, or marginalized communities, and design schemes to cater to their demands and aspirations. This targeted approach aims to mobilize aid from these clusters and sway the electoral outcome in favor of the party announcing the schemes.

The announcement of pre-election social schemes often triggers a competitive environment among political parties. Parties strive to outdo each other by promising more comprehensive or attractive plans to woo voters. This competitive politics can lead to a proliferation of schemes and sometimes result in overemphasizing short-term, populist measures rather than supportable long-term solutions.

Pre-election social schemes serve as powerful political messaging tools. Political parties use these schemes to convey their policy priorities, ideology, and vision for governance. Parties frame their projects to align with their narrative and reinforce their political agenda. The messaging associated with these schemes aims to create an optimistic view and good perception of the party among voters and build trust and credibility.

Political considerations can influence the execution of pre-election social schemes. Schemes may need help with adequate resources, bureaucratic inefficiencies, or political interference. Political dynamics, including government or party priorities changes, can impact these schemes' continuity and functional effectuation, leading to outcome variations.

Pre-election social schemes offer a chance for voters to hold political parties accountable for their promises. Voters evaluate the performance and impact of these schemes when making their electoral choices. Only parties that deliver on their promises or implement schemes effectively may avoid backlash from the electorate, affecting their electoral prospects. While pre-election social plans are often associated with short-term electoral gains, their long-term implications are equally crucial.

The Way Forward

The way forward is to balance providing social welfare and ensuring these schemes are sustainable. This can be done by:

- Targeting social welfare schemes to the neediest people.

- Making sure that social welfare schemes are well-managed and not subject to corruption.

- Educating voters about the long-term consequences of social welfare schemes.

- Encouraging voters to think about the long-term and not just the short-term benefits of these schemes.

- The sustainability and impact of these schemes beyond the election period are crucial for social development.

By taking these steps, we can ensure that social welfare schemes are used to help the poor and marginalized without creating a culture of dependency and sustainability. Parties must ensure that projects are designed and executed with a long-term vision, considering the population's necessity and society's overall welfare.

Understanding the political dynamics of pre-election social schemes is essential for analyzing their intent, implementation, and potential impact. While these schemes can address pressing social issues and benefit targeted groups, it is vital to critically evaluate their effectiveness, sustainability, and alignment with the broader goals of social development.

Chapter 3

The Dynamics of Pre-Election Social Schemes

Political leaders and parties may strategically design or expand welfare programs to appeal to multiple voter segments, particularly those facing economic hardships.

By proposing or implementing popular social schemes, many politicians aspire to attract votes and gain a competitive advantage over their opponents. The political dynamics of pre-election social schemes can be complex and vary from country to country. However, some general or common trends can be observed.

The common trend is that governments often use social schemes to target a particular section of voters. For example, in the United States, the government has several social strategies specifically designed to benefit low-income voters, such as the Supplemental Nutrition Assistance Program (SNAP) and the Earned Income Tax Credit (EITC).

These schemes are seen as a creative way to mobilize low-income voters and increase their turnout on Election Day.

In many countries, social schemes are often used as a way to curry favor with voters and win elections. This is especially true in countries where there is a high level of poverty or inequality. Political parties try to convince voters that they are the only or best to represent their interests by providing swift bonuses to voters, such as food rations, monetary transfers, or healthcare access. However, social schemes can also be seen as a form of vote buying. This is because they are often offered just before elections when voters are most likely to be swayed by short-term benefits.

In addition, social schemes can also be used to target specific groups of voters. For example, a party might offer a plan that provides financial assistance to a community to win their votes. This type of targeting can be very fruitful in winning elections, but it can also lead to accusations of discrimination.

The media can also affect the political dynamics of pre-election social schemes. In some countries, the channel is used to recommend social procedures and convince voters, but However, in other countries, they may point out the potential risks associated with them.

Overall, the political dynamics of pre-election social schemes are complex and can vary from country to country. However, some general trends can be observed. These schemes are often used to favor voters and win elections. Still, they can also be seen as a form of vote buying and can lead to accusations of discrimination. The media can also play a role in recommending or criticizing social schemes.

In addition to announcing new schemes or increasing benefits, governments or political parties may also use social strategies to reward their supporters or punish their opponents. For example, in some countries, the government may impart preferential access to social projects to supporters of the ruling party. Conversely, the government may cut social security payments or make it more difficult to access social schemes for opponents of the ruling party.

The political dynamics of pre-election social schemes in India are complex and multi-faceted. Targeting specific voter demographics, electoral mobilization, party image and popularity, vote bank politics, regional and state-centric dynamics, and political accountability all furnish the formulation and impact of these schemes.

While these schemes address the population's quick requirement, their design and on-ground results are also influenced by the political motivations of parties seeking electoral gains.

Understanding these dynamics is crucial for comprehending the broader socio-political context and the impact of pre-election social schemes on the electoral landscape in India. In the Indian political landscape, pre-election social schemes significantly shape electoral dynamics and influence voter behavior. These schemes, introduced by political parties in the run-up to elections, are aimed at addressing the speedy requisite of the population, accumulating support, and securing electoral victories.

Voting behavior in India and other Asian countries is a diverse topic.

Many different factors can influence how people vote, including:

- Economic factors: In many Asian countries, economic factors significantly determine voting conduct. People who are more economically well-off are more likely to vote, and they are also more likely to vote for the incumbent party.

- Social factors: Social factors such as ethnicity, religion, and caste can also play a role in voting efforts. In some countries, these factors can be very divisive, leading to elevated levels of political polarization.

- Political factors: Political factors such as the level of democracy and the strength of the opposition party can also influence voting practices. In countries with a strong opposition party, people are more likely to vote, and they are also more likely to vote for the opposition party.

- Individual factors: Individual factors such as education, age, and gender can also play a role in voting behaviour. In general, people with more education are more likely to vote, and they are also more likely to vote for the opposition party.

In addition to these factors, a few other factors can influence voting behavior, such as a good communication environment, the level of trust in government, and the electoral system. There are several reasons for this variation. In some countries, such as Japan and South Korea, voter turnout is very high and there is a strong sense of civic duty, and people feel it is their responsibility to vote.

In some countries, including India, Indonesia & few more, several factors can discourage people from voting, such as poverty, illiteracy, and a lack of trust in the government. Nowadays, a lot of research is going on in Asia to understand voting behavior; as the political landscape in Asia continues to evolve, it will be essential to understand the factors that influence how people vote to ensure that elections are fair and representative.

Let's understand some additional insights into voting behavior across Asia:

- Influence of family and friends: In many Asian cultures, family, and friends play a significant role in influencing how people vote. Sometimes, people may feel pressure to vote for the same party as their family or friends.

- Role of the media: The media can also play a significant role in influencing voting behaviour. In some countries, the government tightly controls the media, and it can be used to push the ruling party. In other countries, the press is more independent, and it can enable voters with a range of different viewpoints.

- Rise of social media: social media is becoming increasingly essential in influencing voting behaviour. Social media has been used in many countries to mobilize voters and advertise political change. In other countries, social media has been used sometimes to spread misinformation and disinformation.

Let us again go back to understanding the political dynamics and start with a critical contributor, i.e.

Competitive Populism

Political parties compete to offer attractive schemes and promise to capture voters' attention. This leads to parties engaging in a populist race, vying to outdo one another in announcing welfare programs, subsidies, and value for different fractions of society. Competitive populism creates a political environment where parties vie for the electorate's favor through the allure of immediate usefulness and social welfare measures.

Populist politics has gained traction in recent years, with leaders across the globe adopting populist rhetoric and policies to appeal to the masses. One form of populism that has emerged is competitive populism, where political parties engage in a race to offer populist measures to gain popular support.

Competitive populism can be defined as a spectacle where political parties or leaders engage in a competition to win over voters by offering populist policies and measures. These policies often focus on addressing the people's immediate concerns, such as economic inequality, job creation, social welfare, and nationalism. The core appeal of competitive populism lies in its ability to tap into the grievances and aspirations of the population, promising swift and decisive action to address their concerns.

There are some case studies or examples to understand competitive populism:

- **The United States:** The rise of Donald Trump in the United States is often seen as a case study in competitive populism. Trump's campaign was based on a promise to "drain the swamp" of corrupt politicians in Washington, D.C., and to "Make America Great Again." He appealed to voters who felt that they had been left behind by the economic and political establishment.

- **Brazil:** The rise of Jair Bolsonaro in Brazil is another example of competitive populism. Bolsonaro's campaign was based on a promise to crack down on crime and corruption, and to restore Brazil's traditional values. He appealed to voters who felt that Brazil was being overrun by crime and violence, and that its traditional values were being eroded.

- **Poland**: The rise of the Law and Justice Party (PiS) in Poland is another example of competitive populism. PiS's campaign was based on a promise to protect Polish values and traditions, and to stand up to the European Union. It appealed to voters who felt that Poland was being threatened by globalization and immigration.

- **Hungary**: The rise of Viktor Orbán in Hungary is also seen as a case of competitive populism. Orbán's campaign was based on a promise to defend Hungarian sovereignty and to protect Hungarian jobs. He appealed to voters who felt that Hungary was being taken advantage of by the European Union.

These are just a few examples of competitive populism. It is a growing phenomenon around the world, and it is likely to continue to be a major force in politics in the years to come.

Here are some of the key characteristics of competitive populism:

- **Appeal to "the people"**: Populists often claim to speak for the common people, who they see as being under threat from the elites.

- **Anti-establishment sentiment:** Populists often attack the political establishment, which they see as corrupt and out of touch with the needs of the people.

- **Simple solutions to complex problems:** Populists often offer simple solutions to complex problems, which can be appealing to voters who are frustrated with the status quo.

- **Use of fear and anger:** Populists often use fear and anger to mobilize their supporters. They may scapegoat minority groups or immigrants, or they may play on people's fears about the economy or security.

- **Personalization of politics:** Populists often focus on the personality of the leader, rather than on the policies of the party. They may use charisma and strongman tactics to appeal to voters.

Beyond the mentioned competitive populism is its emphasis on short-term solutions and instant gratification. Political parties engage in a race to promise populist measures, often overlooking such policies' long-term consequences or feasibility.

This short-termism can lead to uncurable economic practices, such as excessive public spending, accumulation of debt, or neglect of structural reforms. Furthermore, competitive populism tends to exploit public sentiment and emotions rather than focusing on evidence-based policymaking. Populist leaders often use charismatic rhetoric, simplistic narratives, and emotional appeals to mobilize without delving into the complexities of the issues. This can lead to policy decisions based on popular sentiment rather than rational analysis, undermining a nation's overall governance and long-term success.

Competitive populism also poses challenges to democratic processes. The intense competition among political parties to outdo each other in offering populist measures can result in degrading political discourse.

Parties may resort to polarizing tactics, divisive rhetoric, and personal attacks to gain an edge over their opponents. This undermines the quality of public debate, erodes trust in institutions, and hampers the ability to find constructive and explicable solutions to complex problems.

Moreover, pursuing competitive populism can significantly affect public finances and socioeconomic stability. The enactment of populist measures without adequate fiscal planning or consideration of long-term consequences can lead to budgetary deficits, inflationary pressures, and economic instability. Such policies may produce short-term relief but can exacerbate underlying structural issues and impede long-term development.

Competitive populism is a type of curiosity that involves political parties engaging in a race to offer populist policies to gain popular support. While it taps into the immediate concerns and aspirations of the people, it often neglects long-term consequences, evidence-based policy-making, and constructive political discourse. The pursuit of competitive populism can pose challenges to democratic processes, governance, and socioeconomic stability. It is essential for political leaders, institutions, and citizens to critically assess the merits and drawbacks of populist measures to ensure supportable and broad-based development.

Let's try to understand how political parties employ various strategies to target multiple voter demographics in their quest to secure electoral support. Understanding different voter groups' diverse prerequisites and aspirations allows parties to effectively tailor their messaging, policies, and campaign tactics to connect with these demographics.

One approach employed by political parties is policy focus.

Parties develop policies and platforms that specifically address the concerns of targeted voter demographics. For instance, parties may propose healthcare, education, employment, or social welfare schemes to appeal to particular groups.

By emphasizing policies that resonate with the targeted demographics, parties wish to gain their trust. For example, a party may prioritize affordable housing initiatives to attract young urban voters while focusing on agricultural reforms to win the devotion of rural farming communities.

Another strategy is the deployment of outreach programs. Political parties conduct targeted outreach programs to connect with specific voter demographics. These programs involve engaging with communities through rallies, town hall meetings, door-to-door campaigns, and community events. By directly interacting with voters, parties can listen to their concerns, address their issues, and establish a personal connection.

These outreach efforts enable parties to understand specific demographics' unique challenges and demonstrate their commitment to resolving them.

Moreover, parties leverage communication channels to target specific voter demographics. They tailor their messaging and campaign advertisements to appeal to particular classes or communities' values, aspirations, and concerns. For example, parties may use social agencies and their platforms to engage with younger voters who are more active online. By employing language, symbols, and visuals that resonate with the targeted demographics, parties aim to create a sense of identification and encourage support.

Targeting specific voter demographics is significant for political parties, allowing them to create a more focused and targeted campaign strategy. By understanding different batches' unique concerns and aspirations, parties can address these issues directly, build trust, and present themselves as champions of various causes.

This targeted approach also helps parties mobilize burden from specific demographics, consolidating their voter base and increasing their chances of electoral success. However, it is crucial to note that while targeting certain voter geographics can help secure support, it should be done with integrity and genuine concern for the well-being of those groups.

Political parties should avoid resorting to divisive tactics or making empty promises solely for electoral gains. Genuine engagement, policy implementation, and accountability are crucial to building long-term trust and ensuring the well-being of all citizens.

Political parties employ various strategies to target certain voter demographics. These strategies include policy focus, outreach programs, and tailored messaging. Targeting distinct geographics allows parties to address different voter groups' unique concerns and aspirations, establish a personal connection, and mobilize support. However, parties must approach demographic targeting with integrity and a genuine commitment to serving the people's interests.

Ultimately, political parties should strive to create a society that caters to the diverse wants of all citizens, irrespective of their demographic characteristics.

There is one more angle to it, and that is electoral mobilization.

Electoral mobilization is a critical aspect of democratic processes involving voters' active participation in elections. It encompasses various strategies and efforts to motivate individuals to exercise their right to vote and participate in the democratic process.

One key aspect of electoral mobilization is voter education. Political parties, civil society organizations, and election commissions undertake campaigns to educate citizens about the importance of voting, the electoral process, and their role in shaping their future through their votes.

Voter education initiatives give information about candidates, party platforms, and election procedures, enabling voters to make informed choices. Electoral mobilization ensures an active and informed electorate by empowering individuals with knowledge.

Campaigns and political rallies are another critical element of electoral mobilization. Political parties organize rallies, public meetings, and door-to-door campaigns to connect with voters, convey their messages, and build support. These activities serve as platforms for candidates to engage with voters, address their concerns, and showcase their policies.

By rallying supporters and generating enthusiasm, campaigns mobilize voters, encouraging them to vote to support the party or candidate. Moreover, grassroots mobilization efforts play a significant role in electoral mobilization. Community-level volunteers, party workers, and activists engage in door-to-door canvassing, phone calls, and local outreach to encourage voter registration, turnout, and support for their preferred candidates.

This personalized approach allows for direct interaction, understanding the specific concerns of voters, and building trust. Grassroots mobilization ensures that everyone feels valued and that their voice matters in the electoral process.

The impact of electoral mobilization is far-reaching. It increases voter turnout, which is vital for the legitimacy and representativeness of elections. When more individuals participate, the election results accurately reflect the people's will. Mobilization efforts also enhance political awareness, encouraging citizens to participate actively in their democracy beyond just voting. By engaging voters, mobilization helps build a sense of ownership and responsibility among citizens toward their nation's governance.

Additionally, electoral mobilization can influence electoral outcomes. Parties that effectively mobilize their loyalty base and persuade undecided voters have a higher chance of securing victory.

Mobilization efforts that resonate with specific voter demographics, such as youth, women, or minority groups, can sway the electoral balance in favor of a particular candidate or party. Mobilization strategies that highlight pressing issues and connect with the electorate's aspirations can significantly impact voter choices.

Electoral mobilization is crucial in democratic processes by encouraging voter participation and engagement. By empowering individuals, fostering political awareness, and ensuring broader representation, electoral mobilization strengthens the foundations of democracy. Political parties, civil society organizations, and citizens must continue to invest in and prioritize efforts to mobilize voters, as active citizen participation is essential for a vibrant and unrestricted democracy.

Managing Party Image and Popularity: Strategies for Political Success

In the realm of politics, the depiction and popularity of political parties play a pivotal role in shaping public perception and determining electoral success. Political parties must carefully manage their party reputation to project a confident and appealing figure to the electorate.

Firstly, Credible communication is a fundamental aspect of managing party representation and popularity. Political parties must craft clear and compelling messages that resonate with the electorate's values, aspirations, and concerns.

They employ various communication channels, including social media, traditional media, public speeches, and party manifestos, to convey their vision, policies, and achievements. By ensuring consistent and coherent messaging, parties can shape public perception, establish credibility, and build a strong party image.

Furthermore, political parties use strategic branding to create a distinct party identity. They develop logos, slogans, and visual representations that encapsulate their core values and resonate with the target audience.

Branding helps parties differentiate themselves from competitors, install a sense of trust and familiarity among voters, and reinforce their party image. Parties often leverage successful party leaders as brand ambassadors, associating their popularity and charisma with the party's values and goals.

Another strategy political parties employ is appropriately utilizing social media and digital platforms. In today's digital age, political parties recognize the significance of online presence in shaping public opinion and engaging with the electorate. Parties actively maintain social media profiles, engage in real-time interactions with supporters, and disseminate information about party initiatives, achievements, and futuristic plans.

By leveraging the power of social media, parties can reach a wider audience, target specific demographics, and shape public discourse. Moreover, political parties actively manage their public appearances and engagement. They participate in public events, community gatherings, and rallies to connect with voters on a personal level. Parties make efforts to be seen as accessible and responsive to public concerns.

Engaging with citizens through town hall meetings, door-to-door campaigns, and public consultations allows parties to address local issues, demonstrate empathy, and build trust. Such direct engagement helps parties manage their image as responsive and accountable representatives of the people.

Additionally, political parties recognize the importance of maintaining a solid and competent leadership team. Parties invest in grooming charismatic leaders who can effectively articulate the party's vision, connect with voters, and inspire confidence. Leaders play a critical role in shaping the party's popularity.

Their attributes, such as credibility, communication skills, and leadership qualities, significantly influence the party's public perception. Parties often emphasize their leader's accomplishments, experience, and ability to deliver on an agreement to enhance party popularity.

Parties also engage in strategic alliances and coalitions to boost their party glory and expand their contract base. By aligning with like-minded parties or influential regional leaders, parties can tap into different voter demographics, consolidate their resources, and present a broader appeal to the electorate.

Alliances also provide opportunities for sharing knowledge, resources, and campaign strategies, increasing the party's visibility and popularity. Furthermore, proper administration and delivery of promises are vital for maintaining party popularity. Parties must prioritize constructive policy implementation, efficient governance, and timely delivery of public services. Fulfilments made during election campaigns help parties build credibility and trust among the electorate.

Political parties employ various strategies to manage their party portrayal and enhance their popularity. Assertive communication, strategic branding, utilization of social media, personal engagement, strong leadership, strategic alliances, and efficient regime are critical elements in managing party image and popularity.

Political parties must recognize the importance of maintaining a confident and appealing party representation to gain public attentiveness and ensure electoral success. By consistently projecting a strong party identity, connecting with voters, and delivering on promises, parties can build trust, credibility, and popularity among the electorate.

As we discuss the political dynamics, how can we forget the vote bank politics?

Vote bank politics is a term used to describe the practice of political parties targeting separate social or religious batches to secure their electoral support. It refers to the strategy of appealing to a particular community's interests, concerns, or aspirations in exchange for their votes.

It often concerns identity-based considerations such as caste, religion, language, or regional affiliations. Parties craft their policies, campaign messages, and even candidate selection based on these considerations to mobilize support from various communities by offering targeted incentives or addressing precise grievances, parties' targets to consolidate a loyal vote bank that can significantly influence electoral outcomes.

One of the significant implications is the potential fragmentation of society along identity lines. When parties prioritize appealing to specific communities, it can create divisions and foster a sense of identity politics.

This can undermine the idea of a united and wide-ranging society, as individuals may perceive their interests as being tied solely to their identity group rather than the collective welfare of the nation. In extreme cases, it can exacerbate social tensions and lead to the marginalization of certain groups.

Moreover, vote bank politics can hinder merit-based policymaking and the overall blooming agenda. Parties may prioritize short-term populist measures that appease communities over long-term, encompassing policies that benefit the entire population.

This can result in skewed resource allocation, neglecting the needs of underrepresented communities. It also discourages many politicians from implementing unpopular but necessary reforms that may be crucial for the nation's overall progress.

Furthermore, vote bank politics can perpetuate clientelism and patronage networks. Parties may distribute favors, monetary incentives, or targeted welfare schemes to gain the loyalty of particular communities.

While this may temporarily benefit the targeted group, it can create a dependency culture and hinder individual empowerment. Moreover, it may lead to corruption, as many politicians exploit the system to maintain their hold on the vote bank. However, it is essential to note that vote bank politics is not inherently harmful or undemocratic. In diverse societies like India, where various communities coexist, it is natural for political parties to consider the interests and aspirations of different groups.

Representing and addressing the concerns of specific communities is an essential aspect of democratic governance. Parties that genuinely advocate for the rights and well-being of marginalized groups can play a conclusive role in the democratic process.

Addressing the challenges posed by vote bank politics requires a multi-faceted approach.

- First, encouraging universal politics that transcends identity-based divisions is crucial. Parties should strive to appeal to all citizens' broader interests and aspirations, emphasizing unity, equality, and shared development. This requires building bridges across communities and fostering a sense of national identity that goes beyond narrow affiliations.

- Second, strengthening institutions and democratic processes can help mitigate the dismissive impact of vote bank politics. Ensuring transparency, accountability, and equal representation within political parties and electoral systems can promote a more complete and merit-based approach. Strong institutions that uphold the rule of law and protect individual rights can help counterbalance the influence of vote bank politics and ensure fair and neutral governance.

- Lastly, enhancing political literacy and citizen awareness is vital. Educating voters about the consequences of identity-based politics, encouraging critical thinking, and pushing civic engagement can empower individuals to make informed choices based on broader considerations. A politically aware and active citizenry can demand accountability from political parties and help steer the political discourse toward development-oriented agendas.

This is a complex circumstance that can have both positive and obstructive implications for democracy.

While it allows parties to represent the interests of various communities, it can also lead to social fragmentation, policy distortion, and patronage networks. Striking a balance between community representation and the broader welfare of the nation is essential. By pushing integrative politics, strengthening institutions, and fostering political awareness, societies can mitigate the challenges posed by vote bank politics and uphold the principles of democracy.

Vote-bank politics and political manipulation are strategies employed by many politicians to secure electoral support by targeting groups based on their identity, social affiliations, or interests. While appealing to specific voter segments is a legitimate aspect of democratic politics, manipulating and exploiting these divisions for short-term gains poses significant challenges to the democratic process.

India being the world's largest democracy, characterized by a vibrant and diverse political landscape. The functioning of democratic systems in India has evolved over the years, reflecting the country's commitment to democratic principles and institutions.

Many political ideologists engage in identity-based rhetoric, making promises or providing preferential treatment to fixed groups, regardless of the broader implications for administration or societal harmony. This approach aims to secure the loyalty of targeted vote banks, potentially at the expense of equitable outcomes and the welfare of the larger population.

Vote-bank politics thrives on exploiting societal divisions, leading to increased polarization along communal, caste, or regional lines. This fragmentation undermines social cohesion, fostering mistrust and hatred among different groups and hindering national integration.

By focusing primarily on appeasing certain vote banks, many politicians may need to address systemic issues such as poverty, education, healthcare, and infrastructure expansion. This neglect perpetuates social and budgetary disparities, particularly for discriminated communities outside the targeted vote banks.

It also diverts policymakers' attention from long-term development and good governance. Rather than focusing on evidence-based policies and unrestricted decision-making, many politicians may prioritize short-term measures aimed at immediate electoral gains, compromising overall forming and practical power.

Many politicians sometimes exploit religious, caste, or ethnic fault lines to mobilize support, leading to the politicization of identity and exacerbating social tensions. This manipulation undermines the democratic ideals of equality, secularism, and social justice.

Vote-bank politics may marginalize groups that do not fit within the targeted vote banks, reducing their political representation and influence. This can perpetuate exclusionary practices and hinder the democratic principle of equal representation and participation.

The emphasis on catering to determined vote banks can distort policy priorities, as decisions are driven by electoral considerations rather than the overall welfare of society. This can lead to suboptimal policy results and hinder robust governance.

The strategic manipulation of identity-based divisions erodes public trust in the political system. When voters perceive that many politicians prioritize electoral gains over their genuine concerns, it undermines faith in the democratic process and weakens civic engagement.

Implementing electoral reforms that speak for transparency, accountability, and ethical conduct can help mitigate the anti-impact of vote-bank politics. This includes measures such as campaign finance reforms, more vigorous enforcement of electoral regulations, and stringent penalties for identity-based incitement. Advocating civic education and political awareness can empower citizens to critically analyze political appeals and make informed choices based on issues and policies rather than succumbing to divisive tactics.

Policymakers should prioritize comprehensive administration, focusing on equitable growth and addressing the needs of all citizens, irrespective of their identity or affiliations. Ensuring broad-based enlargement and welfare measures can reduce the appeal and effectiveness of identity-based vote-bank politics.

Vote-bank politics and political manipulation present significant challenges to democratic systems. The practice undermines social cohesion, perpetuates inequality, distorts policy priorities, and erodes trust in the political process. Addressing these challenges requires a multi-faceted approach, including electoral reforms, civic education, and a commitment to integrative governance. By developing transparency, accountability, and equal representation, societies can foster a political environment that prioritizes the collective welfare of the entire populace over narrow electoral gains.

Beyond this, we also have one cornerstone, i.e., Political Answerability.

Political answerability or accountability is a cornerstone of democratic governance. It refers to the responsibility of political leaders, institutions, and processes to answer to the public, act in the citizens' best interests, and be held liable for their actions.

At its core, political answerability ensures that those in power are answerable to the people they represent. It establishes a system of checks and balances, limiting the potential abuse of power and encouraging clarity, integrity, and responsiveness in governance— political accountability safeguards against corruption, authoritarianism, and the erosion of democratic values.

One prime aspect of political answerability is electoral accountability. Elections enable citizens the opportunity to hold their elected representatives accountable for their actions or inactions. Through the power of the vote, citizens can reward or punish political leaders based on their performance, policies, and adherence to public interests.

Free and fair elections, accompanied by an informed electorate, grant political leaders accountability, and ensure the representation of the people's will. In addition to electoral accountability, mechanisms such as legislative oversight and judicial review play a crucial role in holding governments accountable. As a representative body, the legislature scrutinizes government actions, passes laws, and ensures compliance with constitutional principles.

Through parliamentary committees, hearings, and debates,

lawmakers can examine policies, question government officials, and allow checks on executive power.

Similarly, an independent judiciary acts as a watchdog, interpreting laws, protecting individual rights, and ensuring that government actions align with the Constitution. Judicial review allows citizens and civil society organizations to challenge government decisions in courts, ensuring that the executive branch operates within the bounds of the law. A solid and impartial judiciary strengthens the accountability of political leaders and institutions.

Transparency and access to information are crucial for political accountability. Governments should adopt policies and practices that advocate openness, facilitate the flow of information, and allow citizens to hold officials accountable.

Freedom of the press and a vibrant civil society are essential in this regard, as they pledge independent scrutiny, investigative reporting, and platforms for public debate. Whistle-blower protection laws and mechanisms for citizen participation further enhance transparency and accountability.

Furthermore, political parties have a responsibility to foster internal accountability. Party leaders should be accountable to their members and adhere to democratic principles in candidate selection, policy-making, and decision-making processes. Internal party democracy ensures that party leaders are answerable to their constituents and party platforms align with public interests.

Civil society organizations also play a crucial role in holding political leaders accountable. NGOs, advocacy groups, and grassroots movements act as watchdogs, monitoring government actions, conducting research, and advocating for policy reforms.

They raise awareness, mobilize public opinion, and create platforms for citizen engagement. A free and independent channel acts as a watchdog, exposing corruption, highlighting government failures, and providing a voice for belittled communities.

However, political accountability faces several challenges that need to be addressed. One challenge is the concentration of power in the hands of a few political elites or dominant parties. This can lead to a lack of accountability as power becomes entrenched and unchallenged. Encouraging political pluralism, promoting competitive elections, and strengthening democratic institutions can help mitigate this challenge.

Another challenge is the influence of money and vested interests in politics. Political campaigns funded by wealthy individuals or corporations can compromise the accountability of elected officials, leading to policy decisions that favor special interests over the public good.

Implementing campaign finance reforms, ensuring transparency in political donations, and stimulating public funding of elections can help reduce the undue influence of money in politics. Moreover, boosting citizen engagement and political awareness is crucial for fostering a culture of accountability.

Chapter Four

Positive Effects of Pre-Election Social Schemes: Empowering Communities

India, as a burgeoning democracy and an economic powerhouse, has seen a significant transformation in terms of development and growth. Yet, amidst the skyscrapers, IT parks, and burgeoning middle class, there exists a substantial segment of the population that still struggles with poverty, lack of education, healthcare, and basic amenities. Social schemes targeting these vulnerable sections of society are not just a moral imperative but also a crucial step towards realizing the full potential of the nation.

Bridging the Inequality Gap

India faces stark income inequality. According to various reports, a significant percentage of the nation's wealth is concentrated in the hands of a tiny fraction of the population. Social schemes such as subsidized food programs, direct cash transfers, and employment guarantees aim to redistribute resources more equitably. These schemes act as safety nets for the poor, ensuring that they have access to necessities like food, healthcare, and a source of income.

As per International Labour Organization, Despite the unprecedented worldwide expansion of social protection during the COVID-19 crisis, more than 4 billion people around the world remain entirely unprotected, a new International Labour Organization (ILO) report says.

It finds that the pandemic response was uneven and insufficient, deepening the gap between countries with high- and low-income levels and failing to afford the much-needed social protection that all human beings deserve.

Despite laudable progress in building social protection systems over more than 100 years, most of the world's population is still excluded from any form of social security. Lessons learned from COVID-19 strengthen the case for countries to redouble their efforts to build universal, adequate, and comprehensive social protection systems, including social protection floors.

Despite positive trends in some parts of the world, many countries still face significant challenges in closing social protection gaps to make the human right to social security a reality for all.

Social protection systems operate in a context of high, and sometimes growing, levels of informality and inequality, marked by limited fiscal space, institutional fragmentation and competing priorities, as well as climate change, digital transformation, and demographic shifts.

Changing work and employment relationships, alongside weakened Labour market institutions, have contributed to growing levels of inequality and insecurity and stagnation in Labour incomes in many parts of the world.

Social protection includes access to health care and income security, particularly in relation to old age, unemployment, sickness, disability, work injury, maternity, or loss of a main income earner, as well as for families with children.

The Social schemes can help improve the lives of those in need, increase voter turnout, and build trust between the government and the people. However, it is crucial to ensure that these schemes are implemented fairly and transparently and do not undermine the integrity of the electoral process.

There are some positive or constructive effects that pre-election social schemes can have. First, they can help improve the lives of those most in need. For example, cash transfers can help to reduce poverty and hunger, and job creation programs can help to create employment opportunities.

Second, pre-election social schemes can help to increase voter turnout. When people see that the government is taking steps to improve their lives, they are more likely to turn out to vote. This is especially true for those who are traditionally underrepresented or excluded from the political process.

Third, pre-election social schemes can build trust between the government and the people. When people see that the government is willing to invest in their well-being, they are more likely to have a pragmatic view of the government and its policies.

Social schemes can help to increase social welfare by extending much-needed assistance to poor and vulnerable people. This can lead to a reduction in poverty and inequality, and it can also improve the overall health and well-being of the population. Social schemes can also boost economic growth by enabling a safety net for businesses and workers. This can lead to increased investment and job creation, which can further boost the economy.

Social schemes can also improve public finances by reducing the need for other forms of social welfare, such as unemployment benefits or healthcare subsidies. This can lead to a reduction in government spending, which can help to reduce the deficit or debt. These schemes aim to address multiple communities' socio-economic needs and uplift them through targeted welfare programs and initiatives.

Let's understand this in a more descriptive way.

A significant beneficial effect of social schemes is improving access to necessities and services for needy communities. Many disadvantaged groups, such as people experiencing poverty, women, children, and rural populations, often face barriers in accessing education, healthcare, clean water, sanitation, and housing.

Social schemes can help them overcome these barriers with the necessary resources and infrastructure. By ensuring basic needs are met, these schemes lay the foundation for a better quality of life and enhance the overall well-being of communities.

Education plays a pivotal role in empowering communities and breaking the cycle of poverty. Pre-election social schemes often include initiatives such as scholarships, free textbooks, and mid-day meal programs to increase school enrollment and reduce dropout rates, particularly among poor students. By advocating education, these schemes not only enable children with a chance to acquire knowledge and skills but also open doors to better opportunities and upward social mobility.

Education empowers individuals, allowing them to make informed decisions, participate in the workforce, and shell out to the blooming of their communities. Healthcare is another crucial area where pre-election social schemes can have an incontestable impact. Many underprivileged communities lack access to quality healthcare services, leading to increased morbidity and mortality rates.

Social schemes focusing on healthcare can come up with free or subsidized medical treatment, access to medications, immunization programs, and establishing healthcare infrastructure in remote areas. By improving access to healthcare, these schemes enhance communities' overall health and well-being, reduce healthcare-related financial burdens, and increase life expectancy.

Pre-election social schemes also work toward women's empowerment, specifically who often face multiple forms of discrimination and socio-economic disadvantages. These schemes may include initiatives such as financial assistance for women entrepreneurs, skill progression programs, reservation quotas for women in political representation, and measures to address gender-based violence.

By empowering women, these schemes play a part in gender equality, women's economic empowerment, and their meaningful participation in decision-making processes. Empowered women play a pivotal role in shaping the socio-economic maturity of their communities and breaking gender-based stereotypes.

Furthermore, pre-election social schemes can add value to the spread out of infrastructure in rural and underdeveloped areas. These schemes often include initiatives for road construction, electricity connectivity, access to clean drinking water, irrigation facilities, and the initiation of agricultural infrastructure. By improving infrastructure, these schemes create an enabling environment for economic growth, enhance connectivity, and facilitate the movement of goods and services. This, in turn, stimulates economic activities, increases employment opportunities, and uplifts the standard of living for communities residing in these areas.

Social schemes also anticipate avenues for community participation and empowerment. They often involve the formation of self-help groups, community-based organizations, and cooperative societies. These platforms allow individuals to unite, share resources, exchange knowledge, and collectively address their monetary challenges.

These schemes work for social cohesion, local leadership, and community-driven development by fostering a sense of ownership and collective action. Communities become active stakeholders in their development, taking initiatives and implementing projects catering to their needs and aspirations.

In addition to empowering communities, pre-election social schemes can indisputably impact electoral outcomes. When political parties prioritize the socio-economic well-being of communities, they resonate with the people's aspirations.

By implementing visible social schemes, parties can build trust and credibility among voters, enhancing their chances of electoral success. As voters witness these schemes' tangible welfare, they may be more inclined toward the party in subsequent elections.

However, ensuring pre-election social schemes' transparency, accountability, and sustainability is essential. Proper implementation, monitoring mechanisms, and rigorous evaluation of these schemes are crucial to avoid the misuse of resources and ensure that the intended beneficiaries receive the intended benefits.

Political parties and governments should prioritize long-term planning and comprehensive policies rather than short-term populist measures. This ensures that social schemes' favorable effects are not limited to the pre-election period but continue to empower communities beyond electoral cycles.

Pre-election social schemes have the potential to bring about significant positive effects, particularly in empowering communities and nurturing their overall development. By addressing the socio-economic needs of marginalized groups, these schemes improve access to necessities, enhance educational opportunities, upgrade healthcare, empower women, develop infrastructure, and foster community participation.

Moreover, these schemes can positively influence the electoral effect by building trust and credibility among voters. However, ensuring transparency, accountability, and sustainability in applying these schemes to maximize their meaningful impact is crucial. When designed and implemented effectively, pre-election social strategies can catalyze inclusive growth, social justice, and democratic development.

India has multiple successful schemes, and still, many of us even don't know the name. Let's explore some leading ones.

Education and Skill Development Initiatives

States in India have introduced several education and skill development initiatives and Central government bodies, and many of us still need to learn about them.

Let's explore some of them.

Government of Madhya Pradesh

Scheme Name: Mukhya Mantri Kaushalya Yojana

Launch Year: 2017 onwards.

Facts: More than 2 lac women will be trained under this Scheme annually, applicable in more than 40 districts across Madhya Pradesh. The government of Madhya Pradesh will also provide certification, which the National Council of vocational training will recognize.

Outcome: Under the Scheme, a provision has been made to employ the candidates after passing the training, at least within a month.

Government of Assam

Scheme Name: Northeast Skill Centre

Launch Year: 2016 onwards.

Facts: In October 2016, a Memorandum of Understanding (MoU) was signed between the ITEES and the Assam government to formalize the setting up of a facility. The communique added the courses under which training will be provided were selected after a thorough 'Need-Based Analysis' conducted by ITEES across the State to identify the high-growth potential sectors.

Outcome: The NESC has collaborated with leading industries in multiple job roles to provide employment opportunities for candidates post-training and supporting youths to date.

Government of Odisha

Scheme Name: Shiksha Sanjog

Launch Year: 2020 onwards.

Facts and Figures: The class/subject teachers have created individual

WhatsApp groups with students from different secondary and elementary classes to share study materials. The students of classes II to X are participating in the program.

The program was initiated in the Khordha district on 19th April 2020 and extended to the whole State from 4th May 2020.

A Digital Learning program through WhatsApp group has been implemented to engage students in teaching-learning activities. The subject teachers also remain online to clarify the doubts put by the students in the concerned WhatsApp group.

The Answer key is posted in the evening for self-assessment or assessment with the help of parents. The students have been asked to record all given worksheets with their answers in their notebooks for physical verification by teachers after the reopening of the school.

Outcome: It is heartening to see that many teachers across the State are creating self-recorded video lessons using varieties of TLMs to explain the concepts. Many parents are also engaged with their wards in teaching-learning activities. They have also started interacting with teachers on study matters. The teachers also create different innovative learning materials to understand the concepts easily.

Government of Telangana

Scheme Name: Mana Ooru Mana Badi Scheme

Launch Year: 2022 onwards.

Facts: More than 9000 government schools will be renovated with an approx. Expenditure of Rs. 3000 crores will be extended in a phased manner.

Outcome: This Scheme will give a new lease to government schools which will be going by the brand-new furniture, including dual desks for students, swanky classrooms with pictorial paintings, dining hall, etc.; many would presume it to be a corporate or an international school.

Government of Uttar Pradesh

Scheme Name: Teach Parent Scheme

Launch Year: 2018 onwards.

Facts: Every student teaches at least one elder from their family.

Outcome: Women's literacy in Uttar Pradesh is less than 60 %, and the percentage is far lower in many deep districts. It has been noted that either only one of the parents or both the parents of the students studying in UP government schools are illiterate; therefore, such an initiative will uplift the parents also.

Government of Jammu & Kashmir

Scheme Name: Talash application

Launch Year: 2021 onwards.

Facts: In an effort to track the education of children across the state, J&K's government's education department has set up an app named 'Talaash' so as to get the drop out school kids back to their schools.

Outcome: Under the '*Aao School Chalein* Campaign', the UT administration has enrolled 1.65 lakh children in the last one year. The 'Talaash' app is being used to identify those who had to drop out of schools due to some reasons in the past few years.

Government of Delhi

Scheme Name: Happiness Curriculum

Launch Year: 2018 onwards.

Facts: The Happiness Curriculum was designed over six months by 40 education consultants, teachers, teacher educators, EVGCs, mentor teachers from the Delhi Government, NGOs, and individuals.

Outcome: It improves the mental well-being of pupils. It teaches mindfulness, social-emotional learning, critical thinking, problem-solving, and relationship-building.

Government of Kerala

Scheme Name: Public Education Rejuvenation Campaign (Pothu Vidhyabhyasa Samrakshana Yajnjam)

Launch Year: 2016 onwards.

Facts: The Public Education Rejuvenation Campaign aims to bring a comprehensive revival of the public education system in the State. It suggests the phased up-gradation of the physical and academic infrastructure and the revision of the prevailing curriculum and pedagogy. This Scheme intends to bring international standards to the State's education system by transforming public educational institutions into future centers of academic excellence.

Outcome: Kerala is doing better in the public education sector and has been suggested as a model of emulation for other Indian states. As is well known, Kerala was the first [Indian] State to have achieved universal literacy, with a near-universal school enrolment.

Government of Andhra Pradesh

Scheme Name: Amma Vodi

Launch Year: 2020

Facts: The scheme "Amma Vodi" provides poor mothers (or recognized guardians in the absence of mothers) ₹15,000/- per annum for sending their children to school. The eligible mothers/guardians will be sanctioned ₹ 14000/- which will be deposited directly into the beneficiaries' savings account of the Nationalized Bank/Post Office in January every year until the child passes Class 12th.

Outcome: This Scheme provides financial assistance to families living below the poverty line & also reduces child labor in the State and offers the best education to the children.

Government of Tamilnadu

Scheme Name: Anaivarukkum IIT M initiative

Launch Year: 2023

Facts: Through this scheme 1,000 students would be chosen from government schools to receive guidance in premier institutions such as Indian Institute of Technology, Madras.

Outcome: Such students would receive a monthly stipend of ₹1,000 to ensure that they remain motivated, he said, adding that the candidates chosen under the scheme would receive ₹12,000 as annual stipend during their undergraduate and postgraduate courses. This scheme has been introduced so that government school students do not regret that they did not receive individual training like their peers in private schools.

Government of India

Scheme Name: Pradhan Mantri Kaushal Vikas Yojana (PMKVY)

Launch Year: 2015

Facts: This flagship scheme of the Ministry of Skill Development and Entrepreneurship (MSDE) is implemented by National Skill Development Corporation (NSDC). The objective of this Skill Certification Scheme is to enable Indian youth to take up industry-relevant skill training that will help them in securing a better livelihood.

Outcome: Under CSCM- PMKVY, more than 70 Training Centres are operational, and approximately 30 lacs plus candidates have been trained/undergoing training under STT, RPL, and Special Project.

Healthcare Reforms and Accessibility

Healthcare reform in India has been a topic of extensive debate and action over the past few years. With a vast and diverse population, the challenge lies in ensuring equitable and efficient health services for all.

Some notable initiatives include:

Government of Telangana

Scheme Name: Kanti Velugu

Launch Year: 2018 onwards.

Facts: The program aims to provide comprehensive eye care services to all residents of the State, free of cost, and started with an initial budget of 200 cr, which has been doubled during the Scheme. This Scheme covers universal eye screening, free Spectacles, Surgeries, and Treatment.

Outcome: A whopping 1.60 lakh people turned up at the 522 urban camps and 978 rural camps across the State. All of them were tested. On the first day of the program, the healthcare staff identified 70,256 patients with specific eye-related ailments, and 37,046 patients were provided reading glasses on the spot. For the remaining 33,210 patients, the prescribed spectacles would be provided in due course. About 15,000 healthcare experts would be deployed throughout the State to accomplish the herculean task of ensuring proper eyesight for all. In Hyderabad urban limits, 1,500 teams were deployed, and these teams would undertake eye screening and vision tests for all citizens, irrespective of their age group.

Government of Kerala

Scheme Name: Hridyam

Launch Year: 2017 onwards.

Facts: Special focus on the early management of children with CHD as the management of CHD was crucial to reducing infant mortality in the State. The successful implementation of Hridyam was identified as one of the critical reasons for the steady drop in Kerala's infant mortality rate, which had been stagnant at 12 (per 1,000 live births) for a long time before dropping to 7 in 2018 and later to 6.

Outcome: More than children with CHD have been provided surgical correction of the anomalies. In 2023 alone, 446 children have undergone cardiac surgeries/interventions for correcting CHD. The follow-up care of these children, including their physical and mental development, is being monitored under the Scheme.

Government of Delhi

Scheme Name: Mohalla Clinics

Launch Year: 2017 onwards.

Facts: Delhi Government's Department of Health & Family Welfare and Department of Education came together to synergize and expand their horizons to provide physical and mental health services to children in schools through Aam Aadmi Mohalla Clinics (AAMCs) in schools.

Outcome: According to the Mohalla Clinic's official website, patients can get over 200 free tests. Mohalla Clinics are medical clinics with built-in portable shipping containers. These containers are fully air-conditioned, easily transported, and set up in areas like jhuggi-bastis and narrow streets.

Government of India

Scheme Name: Ayushman Bharat Health Care

Launch Year: 2018 onwards.

Facts: Ayushman Bharat Pradhan Mantri Jan Arogya Yojana is a national public health insurance scheme of the Government of India that aims to provide free access to health insurance coverage for low-income earners in the country.

Outcome: Ayushman Bharat Health Care Scheme Roughly, the bottom 50% of the country qualifies for this Scheme.

Government of Assam

Scheme Name: Dhanwantari

Launch Year: 2021 onwards.

Facts: This Scheme supports home delivery of medicines. The patients can send their prescriptions over the telephone or inform the health workers, and the health department will ensure that it is delivered to them even if it is not on the list of available free medicines.

Outcome: This is the most extensive outreach program any state government takes up at this point.

These healthcare reforms and accessibility schemes reflect the commitment of political parties in India to improve healthcare services, make them more affordable and accessible, and address the health needs of the population.

Focusing on insurance coverage, infrastructure development, preventive measures, and targeted interventions, these initiatives aim to enhance individuals' and communities' overall health and well-being nationwide.

Poverty Alleviation and Financial Inclusion Programs

India has implemented multiple poverty alleviation and financial inclusion programs to uplift the socio-economic conditions of marginalized communities and promote inclusive growth. Some notable initiatives in this regard include:

Government of India

Scheme Name: Pradhan Mantri Awaas Yojana (PMAY)

Launch Year: 2015 onwards and extended till 2024.

Facts: The mission helps the implementing agencies through States/Union Territories (UTs) and Central Nodal Agencies (CNAs) to provide houses to all eligible families/ beneficiaries against the validated demand for homes for more than one crore. As per PMAY(U) guidelines, the size of a house for an Economically Weaker Section (EWS) could be up to 30 sq. mt. carpet area; however, States/UTs have the flexibility to enhance the size of houses in consultation and approval of the Ministry.

Outcome: Under the Pradhan Mantri Awas Yojana – Urban (PMAY-U), More than 120 Lakh houses have been sanctioned, and approx. Sixty lakh houses have been completed.

Government of Telangana

Scheme Name: Dalit Bandhu Scheme

Launch Year: 2021 onwards.

Facts: Under the Scheme, capital assistance of Rs.10,00,000/- will be provided to one person of Scheduled Caste Family to start income-generating activity according to their potential. This assistance is directly from the state government through DBT (Direct Benefit Transfer), without a bank loan with a 100% grant.

Outcome: The State government spent more than 3000 crores under the Dalit Bandhu scheme during the current fiscal, benefiting around 36000 plus Dalit families in the State.

Government of India

Scheme Name: Pradhan Mantri Ujjwala Yojana (PMUY)

Launch Year: 2016 onwards.

Facts: This Scheme provides free LPG (liquefied petroleum gas) connections to women from below-poverty-line households. It aims to promote clean cooking fuel, reduce indoor air pollution, and empower women by providing access to a clean energy source. Under the Scheme, distribute 50 million LPG connections to women of Below Poverty Line families. A budgetary allocation of ₹80 billion was made for the Scheme.

Outcome: As on 1ˢᵗ March 2023, there are 9.59 crore PMUY beneficiaries.

Government of India

Scheme Name: Rashtriya Gram Swaraj Abhiyan Scheme

Launch Year: 2018 onwards.

Facts: The Scheme of RGSA aims to strengthen the capacities of institutions for rural local governance to become more responsive towards local development needs, prepare participatory plans leveraging technology, and efficiently utilize available resources for realizing sustainable solutions to local problems linked to SDGs.

Outcome: The State government spent over 3000 crores under the Dalit Bandhu scheme during the current fiscal year, benefiting approximately 36000 plus Dalit families in the State.

More than Rs 17000 crore have been allocated in the 2023-24 budget.

Government of India

Scheme Name: Pradhan Mantri Kisan Samman Nidhi (PM-KISAN)

Launch Year: 2019 onwards.

Facts: It's an income support scheme for farmers, providing direct financial assistance to small and marginal farmers. It aims to ensure timely support for agricultural activities, enhance farmers' income, and reduce rural poverty.

Outcome: Eligible farmers receive a fixed income support of ₹6,000 per year in three equal installments. The Scheme aims to provide direct income support to small and marginal farmers, helping them meet their agricultural expenses and improve their livelihoods.

India's poverty alleviation and financial inclusion programs reflect the government's commitment to addressing socioeconomic disparities and promoting inclusive development.

By providing income support, access to financial services, employment opportunities, and basic amenities, these initiatives strive to elevate the living conditions of marginalized communities and create pathways out of poverty.

Women Empowerment and Gender Equality Initiatives

India has implemented various women empowerment and gender equality initiatives to address the gender gap, promote women's rights, and ensure their socio-economic empowerment. Some key initiatives in this regard include:

Government of Madhya Pradesh

Scheme Name: Ladli Behen Yojna Scheme

Launch Year: 2021 onwards.

Facts: A scheme has been implemented under which Rs 1000 per month will be given to women. This will be an essential step in the direction of women's health and nutrition, and economic self-reliance.

Outcome: Under the Scheme, the government has distributed more than Rs 2000 crore to approximately one crore beneficiaries.

Government of Telangana

Scheme Name: Kalyana Lakshmi

Launch Year: 2014 onwards.

Facts: Kalyana Lakshmi scheme provides financial assistance to new wedding brides from minority families.

Outcome: A Telangana resident girl, over 18 years of age, belonging to any community with a combined annual income of her parents not exceeding ₹2 lac, is eligible for the Scheme. The financial assistance was increased to more than 1 lac in 2018.

Government of Kerala

Scheme Name: Mangalya – Scheme of Widow Remarriage

Launch Year: 2018 onwards.

Facts: Providing financial assistance of Rs. 25, 000 for eligible widow and divorced women.

Outcome: This Scheme helps maintain the ratio of the total male population of widowed to the female population of widowed, which may affect the overall level of care and support they get from family.

Government of India

Scheme Name: Mahila e-Haat

Launch Year: 2016 onwards.

Facts: Mahila E-Haat is an initiative for meeting the aspirations and needs of women entrepreneurs. It is an online marketing platform for women where participants can display their products. It is an initiative for women nationwide as a part of 'Digital India' and 'Stand Up India' initiatives. The platform has been set up by the Ministry of Women and Child Development, Government of India, under Rashtriya Mahila Kosh (RMK)

Outcome: It promotes women's economic empowerment and provides them a platform to highlight their skills and talents.

Rural Development and Infrastructure Projects

India has initiated various rural development and infrastructure projects to promote inclusive growth, improve the quality of life in rural areas, and bridge the urban-rural divide. Some significant projects in this domain include:

Government of India

Scheme Name: Deen Dayal Upadhyaya Gram Jyoti Yojana

Launch Year: 2015 onwards.

Facts: The Scheme has focused on providing round-the-clock power in rural regions and strengthening the feeder separation of power distribution.

Outcome: Separate electricity transmissions for household and agricultural purposes in the rural regions of India

Government of India

Scheme Name: Pradhan Mantri Fasal Bima Yojana (PMFBY)

Launch Year: 2016 onwards.

Facts: It aims at supporting sustainable production in the agriculture sector by Providing financial support to farmers suffering crop loss/damage arising out of unforeseen events and stabilizing their income to ensure their continued farming.

Outcome: This Scheme encourages farmers to adopt innovative and modern agricultural practices. The Scheme has been focusing on providing round-the-clock power in rural regions and strengthening the feeder separation of power distribution.

Government of India

Scheme Name: Pradhan Mantri Krishi Sinchai Yojana (PMKSY)

Launch Year: 2015 onwards.

Facts & Figures: The primary objective of PMKSY is to achieve convergence of investments in irrigation at the field level, expand cultivable area under assured irrigation, improve on-farm water use efficiency to reduce wastage of water, enhance the adoption of precision-irrigation and other water-saving technologies.

Outcome: Till January 2023, an area of more than 19 lac has been treated, and approximately 46,000 water harvesting structures have been constructed with the creation of a water storage capacity of 400

lakh cubic meter.

Government of India

Scheme Name: Swachh Bharat Abhiyan

Launch Year: 2014 onwards.

Facts: Swachh Bharat Mission – Gramin is abbreviated as SBM-G.As said before, Swachh Bharat Mission (Gramin) is mainly focused in Gramin or rural areas of the nation and would focus on making them open defecation free.

Outcome: According to many surveys and data provided by the government, the rural areas in India are supported with about ten crore toilets under Swachh Bharat Abhiyan.

These rural development and infrastructure projects reflect the government's commitment to uplifting rural communities, improving access to basic amenities, promoting sustainable agriculture, enhancing rural connectivity, and fostering socio-economic development in rural areas.

The necessity for social schemes in India is not just a matter of charity, but a critical component of building a resilient, equitable, and sustainable nation. It's an investment in human capital, which in the long run will contribute significantly to the country's socio-economic development. Therefore, effective implementation and scaling of social schemes is imperative for India's journey towards becoming a just and inclusive society.

Chapter Five

Negative Effects & Economic Consequences Due to Pre-Election Social Schemes: Challenges and Concerns

There are several reasons why promises or commitments made by political powers often make mistakes and later turn into negative or defeatist outcomes.

As per an article published in ORF Online, "The Election Commission of India (ECI), in October 2022, released standard pro-forma to be used by political parties to disclose how they would fund their poll promises. The ECI's directive provoked heated responses from opposition parties, with some of them calling it an "overreach" and an "interference in their democratic rights".

As per the recent publication by RBI and concern raised by Honorable Supreme Court highlights the need for an apex body to address the issue of political parties offering freebies during election campaigns, due to concerns about their economic impact. This comes as various state governments have announced substantial welfare schemes.

A Reserve Bank of India (RBI) report underscores the risks of rising subsidies and debt among states, particularly Punjab, Rajasthan, West Bengal, and Bihar. The excessive focus on freebies, subsidies, and high debt-to-GSDP ratios poses challenges for fiscal sustainability and development.

State governments have introduced over Rs 1 lakh crore in welfare schemes, sparking concerns about the economic implications and sustainability of such practices. RBI's annual report highlights that escalating subsidy burdens are straining state finances, leading to emerging risks such as non-merit freebie expenditures, contingent liabilities, and overdue power distribution companies (discoms).

The RBI's "State Finances: A Risk Analysis" report singles out states like West Bengal, Punjab etc. for their focus on social welfare and warns of potential fiscal stress. Concerns are raised about the negative economic impact of the freebie culture, prompting discussions about its pros and cons. State governments have introduced over Rs 1 lakh crore in welfare schemes, sparking concerns about the economic implications and sustainability of such practices.

RBI's annual report highlights that escalating subsidy burdens are straining state finances, leading to emerging risks such as non-merit freebie expenditures, contingent liabilities, and overdue power distribution companies (discoms).

The debt-GSDP ratio of Punjab is projected to surpass 45% by 2026-27, while states like Rajasthan, Kerala, and West Bengal are predicted to exceed a 35% ratio in the same period. Debt growth in Punjab, Bihar, and West Bengal has outpaced their gross state domestic product growth, indicating an

Some states allocate more than 10% of their revenue expenditure to subsidies, including Gujarat, Punjab, and Chhattisgarh, affecting resource allocation. The RBI report differentiates freebies from public/merit goods, outlining the economic drawbacks of provisions such as free electricity, water, transportation, and loan waivers, which can erode credit culture and distort prices.

The power sector contributes to state governments' financial burdens due to subsidies and capital injections into power distribution companies, with Tamil Nadu, Madhya Pradesh, Rajasthan, and Punjab particularly vulnerable.

The termination of the Centre's GST compensation payout in June 2022 further limits resources for social welfare schemes, necessitating prioritization of expenditures for long-term welfare.

Debt-to-GSDP ratios indicate that Punjab, Rajasthan, Kerala, West Bengal, Bihar, Andhra Pradesh, Jharkhand, Madhya Pradesh, Uttar Pradesh, and Haryana account for a significant portion of state governments' expenditures. States' expenditure trend shows significant spending on revenue over capital expenditure, impacting future growth and interest rates.

Growing trend towards adopting free or subsidized schemes to gain public support requires careful consideration by states to ensure fiscal sustainability and avoid negative economic impacts.

Facts:

- The states prioritize revenue expenditure, limiting fiscal room for capital expenditure.

- High ratio of revenue expenditure to capital outlay confirms the spending trend.

- Revenue expenditure's impact is shorter-lived compared to capital expenditure.

- Imbalanced high revenue expenditure and low capital outlay might lead to reduced growth and increased future interest rates.

- States adopting free or subsidized schemes for public support should be cautious about the financial implications.

- Only financially stable states should implement such schemes to avoid long-term negative effects on state finances.

- Distinguish between freebies and public/merit goods; the latter promote economic benefits like employment programs and education assistance.

- Freebies can undermine credit culture, discourage work ethic, and distort markets, impacting private investments.

- Striking a balance between the financial costs and overall goals is crucial when implementing free or subsidized schemes.

Table 1: Key Fiscal Indicators of States

(Per cent of GSDP)

State	2020-21	2021-22 RE	2022-23 BE	Relative Size of States (in per cent)	2021-22 RE			
	Debt				Interest Payment to Revenue Receipts (Per cent)	Gross Fiscal Deficit	Revenue Deficit	Primary Deficit
Andhra Pradesh	35.5	32.5	32.8		14.3	3.2	1.6	1.4
Bihar	36.7	38.6	38.7		8.6	11.3	5.5	9.2
Chhattisgarh	26.3	26.2			8.0	5.8	0.3	2.1
Gujarat	21.0	19.0			14.2	1.5	0.0	0.2
Haryana	28.0	29.4			20.9	3.0	1.4	0.8
Jharkhand	34.4	33.0	27.0		8.4	3.0	0.1	1.3
Karnataka	22.4	26.6	27.5		14.3	2.8	0.4	1.3
Kerala	37.1	37.0	37.2		18.8	4.2	2.6	1.7
Madhya Pradesh	31.0	31.3	33.3		11.7	4.2	0.6	2.2
Maharashtra	19.6	17.9	18.1		11.4	2.8	1.0	1.5
Odisha	20.0	18.8	18.6		4.3	3.5	3.3	0.0
Punjab	49.1	53.3			21.3	4.6	1.6	0.7
Rajasthan	40.5	39.5	39.8		14.9	5.2	3.0	3.3
Tamil Nadu	26.9	27.4	27.7		21.0	3.8	2.5	1.9
Telangana	25.2	24.7	25.3		11.3	3.9	-0.4	2.4
Uttar Pradesh	29.1	34.9	32.5		11.2	4.3	-1.5	1.8
West Bengal	37.1	34.4	34.2		20.8	3.5	2.2	1.1

← Higher　　　Lower →

Source : RBI Risk analysis Report 2022

Many politicians are often driven by the need to win elections and secure well received support. Pre-election schemes, especially those that promise immediate benefits to certain voter demographics, can be attractive to many politicians as they cater to the desires and demands of the electorate.

However, this populist approach may overlook the long-term consequences and sustainability of such schemes.

In a rush to announce pre-election schemes, many politicians may fail to conduct thorough planning and due diligence. Proper research, feasibility studies, and consultation with experts may be bypassed, leading to poorly designed schemes that lack a solid foundation. Without proper planning, these schemes are more prone to failure and fatalistic outcomes.

Political pressure and competition among parties can drive many politicians to make hasty promises and promises without carefully considering their implications. In the race to outdo each other, many politicians may overlook the practical challenges and limitations of implementing these schemes effectively.

Pre-election schemes often focus on short-term gains and instantaneous electoral benefits. Many politicians may prioritize short-term popularity over long-term evolution and sustainability. This can lead to a neglect of critical areas that require attention, such as infrastructure development, education, healthcare, and job creation.

The absence of robust accountability mechanisms can do mistakes and may release cynical outcomes. Without proper monitoring and evaluation systems in place, many politicians may not be held accountable for their promises and the enforcement of the schemes. This can result in corruption, mismanagement of funds, and a lack of transparency, further exacerbating the uncooperative impact of the schemes.

Several politicians may lack the necessary expertise and technical knowledge to design and implement complex social schemes. Inadequate consultation with domain experts, policymakers, and stakeholders can lead to flawed schemes that do not address the root causes of the issues they aim to solve.

Many politicians may deliberately use pre-election schemes as a means exploit certain voter demographics for their political gain. These schemes may be designed to benefit various communities while neglecting the broader needs and interests of society.

Such exploitation can further deepen social divisions and create a sense of unfairness and dissatisfaction among the populace. It is essential for many politicians to adopt a more cautious and responsible approach when committing to pre-election schemes. They should prioritize long-term development and equitable distribution of resources. Transparency, accountability, and a comprehensive understanding of the socio-economic landscape are crucial in avoiding mistakes and ensuring positive outcomes for the welfare of society.

Pre-election social schemes, often launched by political parties, have become a common phenomenon in many countries, including India. These schemes cater various benefits and welfare programs to the citizens, particularly susceptible sections of society, with the intention of garnering electoral support.

One of the major concerns with pre-election social schemes is their tendency to prioritize short-term gains and populism over long-term sensible development.

Political parties often design these schemes to target certain voter demographics, which can lead to a focus on immediate benefits rather than addressing larger systemic issues. This can hinder the overall progress of the country in the long run. Implementing pre-election social schemes requires significant financial resources. While the intention may be noble, the fiscal burden of such schemes can strain the economy, leading to budgetary deficits and increased government debt.

This can have long-term negative implications for the overall financial health of the country and limit the government's capacity to invest in essential sectors like infrastructure, education, and healthcare.

The rush to launch pre-election social schemes often leads to a lack of proper planning, monitoring, and evaluation mechanisms. This can result in inadequate implementation, corruption, and mismanagement of funds. The absence of robust accountability measures can undermine the effectiveness of these schemes and hinder their intended impact on the targeted beneficiaries.

Pre-election social schemes can be prone to political manipulation and exploitation for electoral gains. Parties may use these schemes to consolidate their vote bank by favoring specific communities or regions. This can create divisions within society and undermine the principles of equitable and inclusive development.

While pre-election social schemes may give immediate comfort to the targeted beneficiaries, there is a risk of creating a culture of dependency on government assistance. This can discourage self-reliance, entrepreneurship, and individual effort. Over time, such dependency can hamper the expansion of skills, creativity, and innovation among the population, hindering long-term rational growth.

Despite the point of targeting susceptible subdivisions of society, pre-election social schemes may suffer from issues of inequitable distribution. There is a possibility of certain categories of the population being left out or receiving lesser satisfaction due to political bias or corruption. This can perpetuate existing social inequalities and marginalize those in need, leading to social unrest and discontent.

The focus on pre-election social schemes can divert attention and resources from critical areas that require urgent attention, such as infrastructure development, job creation, and economic reforms. This can hinder overall progress and limit the government's ability to address pressing issues that are essential for acceptable evolution and long-term growth.

While pre-election social schemes may appear to be well-intentioned, it is important to recognize and address their anti-effects, challenges, and concerns.

There needs to be a balance between short-term electoral gains and long-term societal welfare & policymakers must carefully design and implement social schemes with transparency, accountability, and a focus on long-term impact.

This will help avoid the pitfalls associated with pre-election social schemes and ensure that the welfare of the citizens remains the top priority beyond electoral considerations.

Let's understand more concerns in detail:

Monetary Burden

Pre-election commitments made by many lawmakers, particularly in the form of promises for social schemes and welfare programs, can impose a significant economic burden on the government and the overall economy. These obligations are often driven by political considerations aimed at garnering votes from the electorate. However, the lack of careful planning and consideration of economic realities can lead to adverse consequences.

Pre-election social schemes are sometimes government initiatives, but it's more a political commitment launched with the intention of winning votes by promising immediate service to the electorate. These schemes typically focus on poverty alleviation, healthcare, education, employment, and rural development.

Examples include subsidized food programs, cash transfer schemes, healthcare insurance, and employment guarantee programs. While the objective of these schemes is to address social welfare concerns and reduce inequality, the lack of long-term planning and financial prudence can lead to unintended consequences.

Pre-election social schemes often divert a significant proportion of public resources towards short-term benefits. This can result in misallocation of resources, with inadequate investment in crucial sectors such as infrastructure, education, and research, which are vital for maintaining growth.

Funding pre-election social schemes requires higher government expenditure frequently, leading to an expansion of the fiscal deficit. This deficit is often financed through increased borrowing, which can strain the economy, raise interest rates, and crowd out private investment.

Excessive government spending to finance social schemes can stimulate demand and value add to inflationary pressures in the economy. This inflation erodes the purchasing power of the population, particularly affecting susceptible modules who are the intended beneficiaries of these schemes.

Pre-election social schemes can create an unsuitable fiscal burden by draining public finances. The increased government expenditure without corresponding revenue generation can lead to long-term fiscal imbalances, hindering the government's ability to invest in critical areas such as infrastructure and public services improvement.

The high fiscal burden resulting from pre-election social schemes limits the government's capacity to undertake growth-enhancing policies, such as investments in human capital, technology, and innovation. These policies are essential for long-term economic maturity and can boost productivity and competitiveness.

Continuous reliance on pre-election social schemes can create a dependency syndrome among the beneficiaries, discouraging self-sufficiency and self-reliance. This dependency hampers the instigation of a productive workforce and perpetuates poverty cycles instead of providing provable solutions.

Therefore, it is crucial to base policy decisions on rigorous analysis and evaluation of the social and economic impacts. This includes conducting cost-benefit analyses, considering long-term implications, and ensuring monetary sustainability.

Rather than relying solely on short-term social schemes, emphasis should be placed on investing in human capital phenomenon, including education and skills training, to empower individuals and enhance their employability.

A comprehensive and robust social security system can make provision for verifiable resolution to the susceptible episodes of society without solely depending on pre-election social schemes. This involves targeted welfare programs, insurance coverage, and skill-building initiatives.

Operative capital management is crucial to ensure renewable economic growth. This analysis before elections is essential to ensure responsible economic sovereignty and avoid adverse financial implications.

It should evaluate the feasibility, sustainability, and impact of proposed social schemes, considering the following aspects:

Before implementing any pre-election social scheme, a thorough cost-effectiveness analysis should be conducted. This includes estimating the financial requirements, evaluating the potential benefits, and assessing the long-term impact on the economy. Cost-benefit analysis helps policymakers prioritize schemes that deliver maximum social welfare for the allocated resources.

Adequate budgetary provisions should be made for pre-election social schemes to prevent revenue imbalances. It is crucial to assess the affordability of these schemes within the available taxable space. This involves evaluating revenue streams, exploring alternative financing options, and ensuring that the administration of social schemes does not compromise the overall budgetary health.

Long-term fiscal sustainability should be a primary concern when designing pre-election social schemes. Supportable fiscal management involves analyzing the long-term revenue and expenditure patterns, identifying potential risks, and ensuring that the schemes do not burden future generations with fleeting debt or deficits.

Effective fiscal management requires proper targeting and eligibility criteria for social schemes. Identifying the right beneficiaries based on objective parameters helps in optimizing resource allocation and avoiding leakage and wastage. Implementing robust mechanisms for identifying and verifying beneficiaries can enhance the efficiency and effectiveness of the schemes.

Pre-election social schemes often have cross-sectoral implications. It is essential to assess the potential impact on various sectors of the economy, such as inflation, interest rates, private investment, and overall economic growth. Understanding these interlinkages helps policymakers make informed decisions and mitigate any adverse consequences on the economy.

Continuous monitoring and evaluation of pre-election social schemes are crucial to assess their effectiveness and make necessary adjustments. Regular assessment allows policymakers to identify any fiscal leakages, performance challenges, or unintended consequences. This feedback loop helps in improving the design and execution of schemes over time.

Transparent communication with the public about the fiscal implications of pre-election social schemes is vital. Citizens need to understand the economic trade-offs and the long-term costs associated with these schemes. Propelling fiscal literacy and engaging citizens in the decision-making process can foster responsible fiscal management and ensure public promise for sustainable policies.

Before an election, some parties or even existing governments are often tempted to spend more money in order to win votes. This can lead to unsustainable debt and other problems. However, it is possible to manage the government's finances effectively before an election and still win votes. Implementing and sustaining social schemes can impose substantial financial burdens on governments. The costs vary depending on the scope, coverage, and generosity of the programs.

Social schemes typically include cash transfers, healthcare subsidies, unemployment benefits, education grants, and pension schemes. The costs of these programs encompass both direct expenditures and administrative expenses, such as program management, monitoring, and evaluation.

Effectual money management analysis before elections is crucial to ensure responsible economic governance. Policymakers can make informed decisions regarding pre-election social schemes by conducting cost-effectiveness assessments, evaluating budgetary considerations, ensuring monetary sustainability, and considering multi-sectoral impacts.

This approach will help in avoiding adverse implications, ensure efficient resource allocation, and develop lasting economic growth. Transparency and public awareness about the economic trade-offs associated with these schemes are essential for maintaining public trust and support. The costs of implementing and sustaining social schemes, along with the funding mechanisms and their impact on government budgets, require prudent fiscal management.

Long-term sustainability, economic impact, and productive allocation of resources are critical considerations for governments to ensure the success and longevity of social welfare programs while maintaining financial balance. By striking the right balance, governments can achieve an equitable social welfare system that supports the well-being of their citizens.

Inequitable Distribution of Resources Due to Pre-election Political Schemes

This is one of the most important sections and let's explore this in a detailed way.

The management of resources due to pre-election political schemes is a serious problem that can have several contradictory consequences. These schemes often focus on certain people, such as people experiencing poverty or older people, to win their votes. This can lead to an inequitable distribution of resources, as these groups may receive more benefits than other groups.

One of the main problems with pre-election political schemes is that they can lead to vote buying. This is when voters may be bribed to vote for a particular party or candidate. Vote buying can undermine the democratic process, as it gives an unfair advantage to those who may be willing to pay for votes.

Another problem with pre-election political schemes is that they can lead to corruption. This is when some government officials use their position to enrich themselves or their associates. Corruption can lead to a loss of public trust in government, and it can also make it difficult to deliver essential services.

In addition, pre-election political schemes can also lead to an increase in inequality. This is because the merits of these schemes often go to the wealthy or powerful. At the same time, the poor and marginalized are often left behind. This can lead to a widening gap between the rich and the poor, which can have several negative consequences for society.

Several things can be done to address the problem of inequitable distribution of resources due to pre-election political schemes. These include:

- Ensuring that all citizens have access to information about the schemes. This will help to prevent vote buying and corruption.

- Making sure that the schemes are transparent and accountable. This will help to ensure that the benefits are distributed fairly.

- Targeting the schemes to those who need them most. This will help to reduce inequality.

By taking these steps, it is possible to address the problem of inequitable distribution of resources due to pre-election political schemes and to ensure that everyone has access to the interest of these schemes.

Here are some additional points to consider:

- The timing of the schemes: Pre-election political schemes are often implemented just before an election when voters are most likely to be swayed by short-term benefits.

- The targeting of the schemes: Pre-election political schemes are often targeted at certain people, such as the poor or the elderly. This can lead to an inequitable distribution of resources, as these groups may receive more benefits than other groups.

- The transparency of the schemes: Pre-election political schemes are often not transparent or confusing due to improper communication, which can make it difficult to track the utilities of the schemes and ensure that they are distributed fairly.

It is well understood that Pre-election political schemes are launched to gain electoral fidelity and designed to benefit particular identity or geographical groups, such as caste, religion, or region, with the intention of securing their votes. This selective targeting can marginalize other disadvantaged groups and exacerbate existing social divisions.

The fulfilment of pre-election schemes often diverts resources from critical public services and infrastructure projects. Funds that could have been utilized for education, healthcare, or infrastructure buildout may be redirected towards populist schemes that yield immediate electoral gains.

Focus on politically motivated schemes may result in the neglect of key sectors crucial for inclusive development. Neglecting investments in education, skill development, and job creation can hinder long-term progress and perpetuate socio-economic disparities.

Pre-election schemes aimed at specific vote banks can deepen social divisions and polarize communities along identity lines. This polarizing approach can hinder social cohesion, undermine unity, and exacerbate societal tensions.

The prioritization of certain vote banks can exclude marginalized and susceptible groups from benefiting from public resources and welfare measures. This exclusionary approach perpetuates socio-economic disparities and marginalizes already disadvantaged communities.

Prioritizing schemes based on objective needs assessments and data-driven analysis can ensure a more equitable distribution of resources. Identifying the most deprived areas and marginalized groups allows for targeted interventions to address disparities effectively.

Strengthening transparency and accountability mechanisms in the allocation of schemes can help mitigate favoritism and ensure equitable resource distribution. Open and accessible information about the criteria, selection process, and progress of schemes promotes public trust and reduces the scope for political manipulation.

Emphasizing a detailed planning over short-term electoral gains can help prioritize investments in essential sectors and infrastructure projects. This approach ensures sustainable and inclusive development, benefiting all segments of society.

Engaging citizens in decision-making processes and encouraging their active participation can help ensure a more inclusive and participatory administrative system. It enables marginalized groups to voice their concerns and influence policy agendas, reducing the risk of inequitable distribution of resources.

The inequitable distribution of resources due to pre-election political schemes undermines inclusive and perpetuates socio-economic disparities. Selective targeting, diversion of resources, and the neglect of essential sectors pitch in to an unfair allocation of resources.

Addressing this issue requires a needs-based approach, transparent governance, long-term planning, and active citizen participation. By adopting these measures, policymakers can mitigate the inequitable distribution of resources and work towards building a more inclusive and just society.

A fair and equitable distribution of resources is essential for aiding social cohesion, reducing disparities, and fostering sustainable development. The consequences of these schemes can create challenges in effectively utilizing limited resources, resulting in suboptimal outcomes.

Let's understand and explore the inefficiencies that arise from the consequences of social schemes and their impact on resource allocation.

Opportunity Costs

The economic consequences of social schemes can impose opportunity costs on governments and society. The financial resources allocated to these schemes could have been utilized for alternative purposes such as infrastructure development, education, healthcare, or research and development.

By prioritizing social schemes without considering the opportunity costs, governments may miss out on investments with long-term economic aid and contribute to rational development.

Misallocation of Funds

Social schemes often require substantial financial resources, and if not managed effectively, they can lead to the misallocation of funds.

Inefficient targeting or inadequate monitoring mechanisms can result in reaching those who are not closely in need, diverting resources from the intended beneficiaries. This misallocation of funds reduces the overall impact and effectiveness of the social schemes, as resources are not directed towards the individuals or sectors where they can generate the maximum benefit.

Displacement of Private Investment

The administration of social schemes, particularly those involving subsidies or preferential treatment, can displace private investment in certain sectors. When the government provides financial assistance or incentives to specific industries, it can create distortions in the market, diverting resources away from sectors that would otherwise receive private investment.

This displacement of private investment can hinder overall economic growth and innovation, as resources may be allocated to less productive or less competitive sectors.

Lack of Productive Investments

When a significant portion of resources is allocated to social schemes, there may be a limited allocation for productive investments that promote economic growth.

This can result in a scarcity of funding for critical sectors such as infrastructure, technology, and human capital development. Insufficient investment in these areas can hinder productivity, competitiveness, and innovation, limiting the potential for economic advancement and job creation.

Disincentives to Productivity

Some social schemes inadvertently create disincentives to productivity and work. When dedication is needed without conditions or requirements, individuals may have reduced motivation to seek employment or improve their skills.

This can perpetuate dependency and hinder the progress of a skilled and productive workforce. Inefficient allocation of resources within social schemes can inadvertently discourage self-reliance to long-term welfare dependency.

While social schemes are designed to address social inequalities and help susceptible populations, the economic consequences associated with these schemes can lead to inefficient allocation of resources.

Misallocation of funds, displacement of private investment, missed opportunities for productive investments, and disincentives to productivity are some of the challenges that arise from these economic consequences.

It is crucial for policymakers to carefully consider the allocation of resources within social schemes, ensuring that they are targeted effectively and do not hinder overall economic growth and development. By optimizing resource allocation and striking a balance between social pact and productive investments, governments can enhance the effectiveness and long-term impact of social schemes while pushing economic progress.

Corruption and Mismanagement

Social schemes which are announced pre-elections can be susceptible to corruption and mismanagement, which undermine their effectiveness and perpetuate systemic problems. Funds earmarked for social welfare may be siphoned off through embezzlement, kickbacks, or inflated project costs.

Pre-election social schemes may become tools for political patronage and favoritism. Many politicians may manipulate the selection process, diverting resources to their supporters or vote banks. This politicization undermines merit-based allocation and perpetuates corruption.

Insufficient transparency and weak accountability mechanisms in the imposition of social schemes create an environment conducive to corruption. Lack of clear guidelines, monitoring, and oversight allows for embezzlement and misuse of funds.

Pre-election social schemes are often hastily conceived without proper planning and feasibility studies. This leads to misallocation of resources, inefficient utilization, and fruitless outcomes. Ill-conceived projects may fail to address the actual needs of the target population.

Insufficient expertise and capacity within the implementing agencies can result in mismanagement of pre-election schemes. Inadequate knowledge of program design, monitoring, and evaluation can lead to substandard and poor results.

The focus on pre-election schemes may divert funds and attention away from critical sectors such as healthcare, education, and infrastructure. This mismanagement can hinder overall enhancement and perpetuate social and economic disparities.

- Corruption and mismanagement in pre-election social schemes erode public trust in government institutions. This weakens the effectiveness and legitimacy of democratic systems, hindering good authority and sustainable development.

- Corruption and mismanagement resulted in the wastage of public funds, which could have been utilized for genuine extension and welfare initiatives. This undermines the efficient use of resources and exacerbates economic inefficiencies.

- Corruption and mismanagement in pre-election social schemes undermine the intended objectives of these programs and perpetuate systemic problems. Rent-seeking, politicization, lack of transparency, and misallocation of resources hinder inclusive growth.

The following measures can be implemented to address corruption and mismanagement in pre-election social schemes:

- Strengthening anti-corruption measures: Enforce strict anti-corruption laws, establish independent oversight bodies, and advocate transparency and accountability in resource allocation and implementation.

- Enhancing capacity and expertise: Invest in training and capacity-building of government officials involved in the execution of social schemes to ensure efficient planning, monitoring, and evaluation.

- Citizen participation and social audits: Stimulate citizen participation and social audits to increase transparency and accountability in the implementation of schemes. Empower civil society organizations and citizens to monitor the progress of social schemes.

- Long-term planning and evidence-based policy: Emphasize

long-term planning over short-term electoral gains. Base social schemes on rigorous research need assessments and cost-benefit analysis to ensure valuable utilization of resources.

Dependency Syndrome and Lack of Sustainable Solutions

In many countries around the world, pre-election social schemes have become a common occurrence. These schemes are designed to deliver temporary relief and support to susceptible sections of society, with the aim of accumulating political deal during election campaigns.

However, one major challenge associated with these schemes is the creation of a dependency syndrome among the beneficiaries, leading to a lack of Long-lasting solutions for the long-term welfare of the populace.

Let's understand and explore the detrimental effects of the dependency syndrome and the need for durable solutions in pre-election social schemes.

Pre-election social schemes typically involve the distribution of financial aid, food supplies, healthcare services, or other bonus to targeted groups in society. These schemes are often implemented hastily and with a short-term vision, primarily motivated by political gains. While they may furnish immediate relief, they often fail to address the root causes of poverty and social inequality.

One of the unintended consequences of pre-election social schemes is the creation of a dependency syndrome among the beneficiaries. When individuals become accustomed to receiving handouts without any effort on their part, they may lose motivation to improve their own circumstances.

This dependency syndrome fosters a cycle of reliance on government assistance, inhibiting self-sufficiency and hindering long-term development. Due to the political nature of these schemes, there is often a lack of focus on stable solutions. Many politicians are primarily concerned with short-term popularity and electoral success, leading to a neglect of long-term planning and implementation.

As a result, the schemes may lack proper monitoring, evaluation, and corrective measures, making them worthless in addressing the underlying issues faced by the susceptible sections of society.

Pre-election social schemes are often implemented without proper financial planning, leading to an increased burden on the government's budget.

These schemes can strain public resources, diverting funds from critical sectors such as education, healthcare, and infrastructure development. Moreover, inefficiencies and corruption in the process can further diminish the impact of these schemes, exacerbating the dependency syndrome.

To break the cycle of dependency and foster sustainable development, it is crucial to shift the focus from short-term, politically motivated schemes to long-term solutions. Resilient solutions involve comprehensive strategies that address the root causes of poverty, such as education, skill development, job creation, and social empowerment. By encouraging self-reliance and fostering an enabling environment, it can lead to long-lasting improvements in the lives of the susceptible population.

Dependency syndrome and the lack of permanent solutions in pre-election social schemes pose significant challenges to the welfare of societies. These schemes, although designed for temporary relief, often perpetuate dependency, and hinder long-term development. It is imperative for policymakers to prioritize durable solutions that address the root causes of social inequality and promote self-sufficiency.

By doing so, governments can ensure the well-being and empowerment of their citizens beyond election cycles, fostering inclusive and resilient societies.

Let's Try to Understand the Economic Consequences

Social schemes have significant economic consequences for countries across the world. While they play a vital role in poverty reduction, human capital development, and social well-being, it is important to carefully manage the economic implications associated with these programs.

Striking a balance between provisioning necessary support and avoiding work disincentives, ensuring fiscal sustainability, and addressing income inequality are key considerations. By carefully designing, implementing, and evaluating social schemes, countries can harness their potential to create a more inclusive and prosperous society.

Implementing social schemes imposes financial obligations on governments. The provision of social benefits, such as healthcare, education, or social assistance, requires substantial financial resources. Social schemes often lead to increased government spending, which can strain fiscal budgets.

Governments must carefully manage their finances to ensure the long-term sustainability of these schemes, as excessive spending or inefficient allocation of resources may lead to money deficits, public debt, and potential macroeconomic instability.

The economic consequences of addressing income inequality through social schemes can have spillover effects. Reduced inequality can enhance social cohesion, promote trust, and foster an environment conducive to economic growth and innovation.

Social schemes that focus on poverty reduction and income redistribution can also enhance domestic demand and stimulate economic activity.

One of the primary concerns associated with social schemes is the strain they impose on government budgets. Implementing and maintaining these schemes requires substantial financial resources, including funding for welfare programs, subsidies, and targeted assistance. The increased expenditure on social schemes can lead to budgetary deficits, reduced fiscal space for other essential sectors, and a potential burden on future generations if not managed effectively. Social schemes often involve the provision of subsidies, grants, or preferential treatment to specific groups or industries. While these measures aim to promote equality and social welfare, they can inadvertently distort market incentives and create economic inefficiencies.

For instance, excessive subsidies can lead to an overreliance on government support, disincentivizing self-sufficiency and hindering the generation of competitive industries. Such disruptions can weaken market mechanisms and hamper overall economic growth.

To finance social schemes, governments often resort to increased taxation or reallocation of existing resources. Higher taxes can negatively impact economic productivity and discourage investment and entrepreneurship.

Moreover, when social schemes deliver substantial benefits, they may create disincentives to work or seek employment, as individuals may perceive greater economic interest from relying solely on government assistance. This fact can lead to reduced labor force participation, decreased productivity, and long-term economic stagnation.

Social schemes, if not designed and implemented carefully, can inadvertently foster a dependency syndrome among beneficiaries. When individuals become reliant on continuous government support, they may lose the motivation to improve their own circumstances and seek self-sufficiency. This dependency syndrome can create welfare traps, wherein individuals remain trapped in poverty cycles due to limited access to opportunities and the disincentive to break free from government assistance.

Social schemes face the challenge of moral hazard, wherein the provision of assistance may lead to reckless behavior or misuse of funds. Individuals may engage in fraudulent activities to exploit the system, resulting in wastage of resources and diverting help, away from those precisely in need.

Inefficient administration processes and inadequate monitoring mechanisms can further exacerbate the risk of fraud, undermining the intended economic impact of the schemes.

Social schemes undoubtedly play a crucial role in addressing socio-economic inequalities and improving the lives of susceptible populations. However, policymakers must carefully consider and address the economic consequences that arise from the setup of these schemes.

Balancing the budgetary strain, market disruptions, disincentives to work, dependency syndrome, and the risk of fraud is essential to ensure the long-term sustainability and effectiveness of social schemes. By designing well-targeted, efficient, and transparent programs, governments can mitigate the challenges and concerns associated with social schemes, fostering economic growth and societal well-being.

As per an article published by OECD, the COVID-19 pandemic has caused a significant deterioration in public finances, adding to pre-existing strains from long-term structural challenges, including population ageing, climate change, rising inequality, digitalization, and automation.

Containment measures, increased government spending and lower tax revenues have driven an increase in budget deficits and government debt, which, as a percentage of GDP, has reached its highest levels over the past several decades.

While current interest payments on sovereign debt are manageable for most countries due to low bond yields and accommodative monetary policy, maintaining high debt increases vulnerability to interest rate increases and growth slowdowns and raises debt rollover risks.

Governments implement social schemes to address social

inequality and poverty and help susceptible sections of society. While these schemes aim to improve the well-being of the populace, they often impose a significant fiscal burden and create budgetary pressures on governments.

Implementing and sustaining social schemes require substantial financial resources. Governments allocate funds for various welfare programs, subsidies, grants, and direct assistance to targeted groups.

As the number and scope of social schemes expand, the overall expenditure on these programs increases, putting strain on government budgets. The rising costs associated with social schemes can lead to budget deficits, increased borrowing, or reduced funding for other essential sectors such as education, healthcare, and infrastructure.

One of the challenges of social schemes is the unpredictability of costs. The demand for assistance and the number of beneficiaries can fluctuate, making it challenging to accurately forecast the financial requirements.

Unforeseen circumstances, such as economic downturns or natural disasters, can lead to sudden spikes in the need for social support, further adding to the monetary burden. Governments must be prepared to allocate additional funds or adjust budgets accordingly, which can strain financial resources and disrupt long-term planning.

The money burden imposed by social schemes can have significant opportunity costs. The resources allocated to fund social programs could have been utilized for alternative purposes, such as investment in infrastructure, education, or research and development.

When a large portion of the budget is allocated to social schemes, it limits the government's ability to invest in other sectors that helps in long-term economic growth and development. This trade-off between social spending and investment in productive sectors poses a challenge for policymakers.

To finance the capital burden of social schemes, governments often resort to borrowing, which can lead to a rise in public debt. Increased debt levels can have adverse consequences, such as higher interest payments, reduced creditworthiness, and limitations on future borrowing capacity.

High debt servicing costs can further strain government budgets and divert funds from productive investments, perpetuating a cycle of revenue pressure. Ensuring the long-term sustainability of social schemes is crucial to mitigate the fiscal burden and budgetary pressures. Governments must adopt measures to balance the financial responsibility of social programs with revenue generation and economic growth.

This can include exploring alternative funding sources, improving tax collection mechanisms, enhancing efficiency in the delivery of social services, and periodically evaluating the effectiveness of existing schemes. Self-sustaining funding models can alleviate budgetary pressures and enable governments to support without compromising economic stability.

Social schemes are vital for addressing social inequalities and improving the well-being of susceptible sections of society. However, the fiscal burden and budgetary pressures associated with these schemes pose significant challenges for governments.

Striking a balance between social spending and overall budgetary requirements is crucial to ensure the long-term sustainability of social schemes. Governments need to adopt prudent capital management, explore alternative funding sources, and prioritize investments that foster economic growth, thus alleviating the tax burden while continuing to enable necessary compliance to those in need.

Let's explore the disruption side of the story.

Disruption of Market Mechanisms Due to Social Schemes

Social schemes often involve the provision of subsidies or price controls to make essential goods and services more affordable for targeted populations. While the intention is to improve accessibility and affordability, these interventions can distort price signals in the market.

Subsidies can artificially lower prices, leading to increased demand and potential supply shortages. The economic consequences of social schemes can reduce market competition. When the government provides preferential treatment or grants exclusive contracts to certain suppliers or industries, it can create barriers to entry and limit competition.

This reduced competition hampers innovation, inhibits the entry of new players, and stifles market dynamism. Without competition, market forces are weakened, leading to suboptimal outcomes and limited choices for consumers.

Social schemes can result in the misallocation of resources within the economy. When the government allocates significant resources to fund social programs, it diverts resources away from other sectors that may have higher productivity or growth potential.

This misallocation can lead to inefficiencies, as resources may not be directed towards their most productive uses. The misallocation of resources hampers overall economic performance and can impede long-term growth prospects.

Social schemes can introduce distortions in market dynamics. For example, when governments impose quotas or preferential treatment for specific groups, it can disrupt supply and demand patterns.

These distortions can result in imbalances, such as oversupply or undersupply of goods or services, leading to market inefficiencies. Distortions can also create a lack of alignment between consumer preferences and the products or services available in the market.

Disruptions caused by social schemes can create disincentives for entrepreneurship and innovation. When the government heavily regulates or controls certain sectors through social schemes, it can discourage entrepreneurial activities.

Excessive regulations, administrative burdens, and reduced market opportunities can deter individuals from starting new businesses or pursuing innovative ventures. This lack of entrepreneurial spirit stifles economic dynamism and hampers the emergence of new ideas and industries. While social schemes serve important social objectives, the economic consequences can disrupt market mechanisms, leading to unintended consequences and challenges.

Distorted price signals, reduced market competition, resource misallocation, market distortions, and disincentives to entrepreneurship and innovation are some of the disruptions that can occur. Policymakers need to carefully consider the potential economic impacts and unintended consequences when designing and implementing social schemes.

Striking a balance between social objectives and market dynamics is crucial to ensure regenerative economic growth, market efficiency, and the promotion of entrepreneurship and innovation.

By fostering competition, reducing market distortions, and boosting policies that encourage productivity and efficiency, governments can mitigate the disruptive effects of social schemes on market mechanisms and foster a thriving, inclusive economy.

Distorted Incentives and Market Distortions Due to Social Schemes

Let's explore the distorted incentives and market distortions that can result from social schemes and their implications.

- **Moral Hazard and Reduced Work Incentives:**

Social schemes that grant financial assistance or benefits without conditions or requirements can create moral hazards and reduce work incentives.

When individuals receive assistance without being required to actively seek employment or improve their skills, it can lead to a disincentive to work or pursue economic self-sufficiency.

This can perpetuate dependency on social schemes and hinder individuals' motivation to participate fully in the Labour market, resulting in reduced productivity and economic growth.

- **Market Substitution and Crowding Out**

The presence of social schemes can lead to market substitution and crowd out private sector initiatives. For example, when the government directly provides goods or services that are traditionally offered by the private sector, it can undermine the viability of private businesses in those sectors. This substitution effect can distort market dynamics, reduce competition, and impede innovation and efficiency. Additionally, the availability of free or heavily subsidized goods or services through social schemes can discourage private-sector investment and reduce opportunities for entrepreneurship.

- **Price Distortions and Inefficient Resource Allocation**

Social schemes often involve price interventions, such as subsidies or price controls, to make goods and services more affordable for targeted populations.

While this aims to improve accessibility, it can lead to price distortions in the market. Subsidies can artificially lower prices, resulting in increased demand, supply shortages, and inefficient resource allocation.

Market forces and price mechanisms become less beneficial in allocating resources efficiently, potentially leading to market imbalances and economic inefficiencies.

- **Reduced Market Competition**

Social schemes can reduce market competition by dispensing preferential treatment or exclusive contracts to specific entities.

One example of a social scheme in India that can potentially reduce market competition by imparting preferential treatment is the reservation system in education and government jobs based on caste.

This reduces opportunities for new entrants and stifles competition, leading to monopolistic or oligopolistic market structures.

Reduced competition hampers innovation, limits consumer choices, and can result in higher prices and lower-quality products or services. The lack of market competition erodes market efficiency and hinders overall economic development.

- **Distorted Investment Priorities**

The presence of social schemes can influence investment priorities and distort resource allocation. Governments may prioritize allocating resources to social schemes, potentially at the expense of critical sectors such as infrastructure development, research and development, or education.

This can impede long-term economic growth and limit the creation of stable employment opportunities. Distorted investment priorities hinder productivity and innovation, undermining the overall competitiveness and potential of an economy.

Social schemes, while well-intentioned, can create distorted incentives and market distortions that have unintended economic consequences.

Moral hazard, reduced work incentives, market substitution, price distortions, reduced market competition, and distorted investment priorities are among the challenges that can arise.

As per RBI the recent economic crisis in neighboring Sri Lanka is a reminder of the critical importance of public debt sustainability. The fiscal conditions among states in India are showing warning signs of building stress. The slowdown in own tax revenue, a high share of committed expenditure and rising subsidy burden have stretched state government finances exacerbated by COVID-19.

For the five most indebted states, the debt stock is no longer sustainable, as the debt growth has outpaced their GSDP growth in the last five years. New sources of risks have emerged relaunch of the old pension scheme by some states; rising expenditure on non-merit freebies; expanding contingent liabilities; and the ballooning overdue of DISCOMs - warranting strategic corrective measures.

Stress tests show that the fiscal conditions of the most indebted state governments are expected to deteriorate further, with their debt-GSDP ratio likely to remain above 35 per cent in 2026-27.

As a corrective measure, the state governments must restrict their revenue expenses by cutting down expenditure on non-merit goods in the near term. In the medium term, these states need to put efforts towards stabilizing debt levels.

Further, considering the power sector ,large scale reforms in power distribution sector would enable the DISCOMs to reduce losses and make them financially sustainable and operationally efficient. In the long term, increasing the share of capital outlays in the total expenditure will help create long-term assets, generate revenue, and boost operational efficiency.

Alongside, state governments need to conduct fiscal risk analyses and stress test their debt profiles regularly to be able to put in place provisioning and other specific risk mitigation strategies to manage fiscal risks efficiently.

Policymakers must carefully design and implement social schemes, considering their potential impact on market mechanisms and avoiding unintended distortions. Balancing social objectives with market efficiency, competition, and entrepreneurship is essential for fostering Long-lasting economic growth and ensuring the effectiveness and long-term impact of social schemes.

Chapter Six

Balancing Political Commitments and Financial Stability

The decisions made by policymakers in India have far-reaching consequences, impacting the country's political landscape and overall economic well-being.

Political commitments or resolutions in India encompass a wide array of promises made by political parties during elections and throughout their tenure. These arrangements often focus on addressing social welfare, poverty alleviation, employment generation, infrastructure development, and reducing regional disparities.

Economic or financial stability is vital for India's sustained growth and development. The country has witnessed substantial economic reforms since the early 1990s, emphasizing liberalization, privatization, and globalization.

Maintaining a stable macroeconomic environment, characterized by low inflation, financial discipline, a favorable investment climate, and sustainable growth, is crucial for attracting investments, fostering business growth, and improving living standards.

The interplay between political fulfillment and economic stability in India is intricate. On the one hand, fulfilling political commitments can add to social welfare and inclusive development, thus strengthening the government's mandate.

On the other hand, hasty or unsustainable commitments can strain the economy, leading to imbalances in public debt and inflationary pressures. It becomes essential for policymakers to strike a balance to avoid detrimental consequences.

Balancing political commitments and economic stability necessitates trade-offs and prioritization. Policymakers must assess political obligations' feasibility, economic impact, and sustainability. It involves carefully prioritizing initiatives, aligning them with long-term financial goals, and considering their potential effects on the fiscal deficit, inflation, and overall economic stability. Prioritization allows for a realistic commitment without jeopardizing macroeconomic fundamentals.

Engaging with stakeholders is critical to achieving the delicate balance between political commitments and economic stability. Collaboration with economists, business leaders, think tanks, and civil society organizations ensure that policy decisions are evidence-based, grounded in economic realities, and aligned with the population's needs. This consultative approach minimizes the risk of pursuing short-term political gains at the expense of long-term financial stability.

Examples from India's experience:

India's journey of balancing political commitments and economic stability offers valuable examples. Although politically challenging, the Goods and Services Tax (GST) implementation aimed to streamline the tax structure, enhance revenue collection, and foster economic integration.

Similarly, initiatives such as the Make in India campaign and Digital India reflect efforts to align political fulfilments with economic growth and technological advancements.

Balancing political commitments and economic stability is a complex task faced by governments worldwide, including India. In India, striking this balance requires judicious prioritization, evidence-based decision-making, and stakeholder collaboration.

By carefully assessing the economic impact of political aspirations and ensuring their sustainability, policymakers can promote inclusive growth, enhance social welfare, and maintain a stable economic environment. Achieving this equilibrium is crucial for India's continued progress and the well-being of its citizens.

The Role of Evidence-Based Policy Making

Evidence-based policymaking is a systematic approach that emphasizes the use of rigorous research, data, and analysis to inform and shape policy decisions. It strives to bridge the gap between theory and practice, enabling policymakers to make informed choices based on empirical evidence rather than ideological or intuitive assumptions.

Evidence-based policymaking is founded on the idea that policies should be grounded in credible evidence, systematically collected, and analyzed. This approach requires policymakers to identify policy issues, review existing research, conduct new studies if needed, and use the findings to inform policy design, implementation, and evaluation. This approach aims to enhance public policy effectiveness, efficiency, and accountability by emphasizing the importance of evidence.

Benefits of Evidence-Based Policy Making:

- **Improved Decision-Making:** Evidence-based policymaking allows policymakers to make well-informed decisions, minimizing the reliance on personal biases or anecdotal evidence. It helps identify the most operative and cost-efficient policy options based on rigorous analysis and evaluation of available evidence.

- **Increased Transparency and Accountability:** By explicitly linking policies to empirical evidence, evidence-based approaches enhance transparency and accountability in governance.

Policymakers can justify their decisions to stakeholders, ensuring that policy choices are based on objective facts rather than political expediency or personal interests.

- **Enhanced Policy Effectiveness:** Evidence-based policymaking increases the likelihood of policies achieving their desired outcomes. By identifying the root causes of problems, policymakers can design targeted interventions that address the underlying issues, leading to more helpful solutions and positive societal impacts.

- **Resource Allocation Efficiency:** Evidence-based policymaking helps optimize resource allocation by identifying the interventions or programs that yield the highest return on investment. This approach minimizes wasteful spending on purposeless policies and directs resources towards initiatives with proven efficacy, maximizing the impact of public expenditure.

- **Long-Term Sustainability:** By considering the long-term consequences of policies, evidence-based approaches promote enduring development. Policymakers can anticipate potential unintended effects and adjust their strategies, accordingly, ensuring that procedures are productive in the short term and subscribe to long-term societal well-being.

Challenges and Limitations:

While evidence-based policymaking offers significant benefits, it faces challenges and limitations:

- **Data Availability and Quality:** Access to reliable and relevant data is crucial for evidence-based policymaking. However, in some cases, data may be limited, outdated, or subject to biases. Policymakers must address data gaps and invest in robust data collection and analysis infrastructure to ensure accurate and comprehensive evidence.

- **Complexity and Time Constraints:** Policy issues are often multifaceted and complex, requiring a comprehensive understanding of various factors and their interrelationships. Conducting rigorous research and analysis can take time, which may clash with the need for quick policy responses. Policymakers must strike a balance between evidence generation and timely decision-making.

- **Politics and Public Opinion:** Policy decisions are influenced by political considerations and public opinion, which may not always align with the evidence. Policymakers must navigate these dynamics, communicate the rationale behind evidence-based decisions effectively, and build public trust in the value of empirical evidence.

- **Interdisciplinary Collaboration:** Evidence-based policymaking often requires collaboration across multiple disciplines and sectors. Bridging the gap between researchers, policymakers, and practitioners can be challenging, as they may have different priorities, languages, and approaches. Encouraging interdisciplinary collaboration and knowledge exchange is essential for effective evidence-based policymaking.

Promoting Evidence-Based Policymaking, let's explore some strategies.

- **Strengthening Research Capacities:** Governments should invest in research institutions, think tanks and academic collaborations to enhance the capacity to generate high-quality evidence. This includes funding research projects, promoting data sharing, and fostering partnerships between researchers and policymakers.

- **Creating a Culture of Evidence Use:** Policymakers must prioritize evidence and create a culture that values research and analysis. This can be achieved through training programs, knowledge-sharing platforms, and institutionalizing mechanisms for evidence integration into policy processes.

- **Engaging Stakeholders:** Collaboration and stakeholder engagement are crucial for evidence-based policymaking. Policymakers can access diverse perspectives, ensure relevance, and build public devotion to evidence-based decisions by involving experts, civil society organizations, and affected communities.

- **Embedding Evaluation Mechanisms:** Incorporating monitoring and evaluation processes into policy allows policymakers to assess the effectiveness and impact of policies. Regular evaluations dispense feedback on policy outcomes, identify areas for improvement, and inform future policy iterations.

Evidence-based policymaking is vital for promoting well-founded governance, informed decision-making, and Continuous development. Governments can improve public policy efficiency, transparency, and accountability by basing policy choices on rigorous research and analysis.

While challenges exist, efforts to strengthen research capacities, create a culture of evidence use, engage stakeholders, and embed evaluation mechanisms can help overcome these obstacles. Ultimately, evidence-based policymaking empowers governments to tackle complex societal challenges and achieve better outcomes for their citizens.

Ensuring Integrity and Transparency in Social Schemes

To ensure social schemes & programs' effectiveness and integrity, integrity, and transparency must be paramount.

Accountability & integrity holds responsible parties answerable for their actions and ensures that public resources are utilized efficiently. Transparency provides that information regarding program design, implementation, and outcomes is readily available to the public.

Accountability & integrity plays a pivotal role in social schemes for several reasons. Firstly, it promotes responsible decision-making and prevents misuse of public funds. When individuals and institutions involved in social systems are held accountable, they are more likely to act in the best interest of the beneficiaries, ensuring that resources are utilized effectively. Secondly, accountability helps identify and rectify any potential corruption or malpractices within the system. Establishing clear lines of responsibility and oversight mechanisms makes detecting and addressing fraudulent activities easier.

Lastly, accountability builds trust between the government, program implementers, and the public. When citizens are confident that their contributions are being used for their intended purposes, they are more likely to participate in social schemes.

Transparency is a fundamental aspect of ensuring the credibility and effectiveness of social schemes. It involves making information accessible to the public, facilitating an open flow of communication, and fostering trust.

By encouraging transparency, governments and implementing agencies can enhance public participation, ensure fairness, and facilitate informed decision-making. Transparency allows citizens to evaluate the performance and impact of social schemes, enabling them to share feedback and hold stakeholders accountable.

Transparency can be achieved through various means.

- First, governments can ensure that program guidelines, eligibility criteria, and processes are communicated to the public. This includes allowing information through easily accessible platforms such as websites, public meetings, and community outreach programs.
- Second, regular reporting and disclosure of financial

information related to social schemes should be mandatory. This includes detailed budgets, expenditure reports, and audits made available to the public.

- Third, establishing mechanisms for public feedback, such as complaint redressal systems and citizen helplines, can enhance transparency by encouraging individuals to voice their concerns or deliver suggestions for improvement.

- Finally, engaging independent organizations, civil society, and the media in monitoring and evaluating social schemes can provide an external check on their result-oriented outcomes.

A better and more robust administrative mechanism in social schemes will strengthen the entire ecosystem.

First and foremost, transparent communication will enhance responsibility and reporting, ensuring that each party involved understands its role and obligations. This includes defining the responsibilities of government departments, implementing agencies, and other stakeholders. Additionally, performance indicators and targets should be set, allowing for the evaluation of progress and outcomes. These indicators should be measurable, time-bound, and aligned with the overall objectives of the social scheme.

Regular monitoring and evaluation are crucial for accountability. This can be achieved by establishing dedicated monitoring units or independent oversight bodies responsible for assessing the implementation of social schemes.

These units should have the Authority to investigate complaints, conduct audits, and suggest recommendations for improvement. Moreover, conducting periodic external evaluations of social schemes by independent experts can give valuable insights and ensure objectivity.

Legal and regulatory frameworks play a vital role in ensuring accountability. Governments should establish laws and regulations that clearly define the roles, responsibilities, and ethical standards for all parties involved in social schemes. These laws should also include provisions for sanctions and penalties for non-compliance and misconduct.

Accountability and transparency are essential pillars in ensuring the success and sustainability of social schemes. By fostering accountability, we can prevent misuse of public resources, detect, and rectify corruption, and build trust among stakeholders.

Conversely, transparency enables citizens to actively participate, evaluate, and share feedback on social schemes.

Governments and implementing agencies must prioritize accountability and transparency by adopting robust mechanisms such as clear guidelines, regular reporting, public feedback channels, and independent monitoring and evaluation. Only through such measures can we ensure that social schemes effectively address the needs of vulnerable populations and achieve their intended goals.

Strengthen Monitoring and Evaluation Mechanisms

India, as a democratic nation, faces the challenge of balancing political responsibilities and economic stability. The government's social and economic policies, such as welfare schemes and infrastructure expansion programs, are crucial for fulfilling political promises and improving citizens' lives.

However, ensuring these policies are effectively implemented and add value to long-term economic stability requires intense monitoring and evaluation mechanisms.

Monitoring and evaluation are vital in balancing India's political engagements and economic stability. Let's understand through some strategies.

- Productive monitoring helps track the progress and policies, ensuring they align with the government's political commitments. Policymakers can identify gaps or challenges hindering the desired outcomes by monitoring the executive process. Evaluation, on the other hand, assesses the impact and effectiveness of policies. It helps determine whether the intended objectives are achieved and provides insights into the necessary adjustments or improvements.

- Evaluation help ensure economic stability by assessing the financial implications of policies. This includes analyzing the cost-effectiveness of programs, identifying potential fiscal risks, and evaluating the overall impact on the economy. By conducting rigorous evaluations, policymakers can make informed decisions regarding the allocation of resources, ensuring that public funds are utilized efficiently and in a manner that supports long-term economic stability.

- There should be a clear mandate and policy framework for monitoring and evaluation across all government departments. This includes establishing guidelines, standards, and procedures for assessing and monitoring progress. Ensuring that monitoring and evaluation are integrated into the policy cycle from the initial design phase to the assessment stage is essential.

- Investing in capacity-building initiatives is crucial. This involves dispensing training and technical resolution to government officials and stakeholders involved in monitoring and evaluation activities. Building a pool of skilled evaluators and fostering a culture of evidence-based decision-making can enhance the effectiveness of these mechanisms.

- Fostering partnerships and collaborations with academic institutions, civil society organizations, and international agencies can bring diverse perspectives and expertise to the monitoring and evaluation process. These partnerships can be instrumental to robust evaluation methodologies, data collection techniques, and knowledge-sharing platforms.

- Pushing transparency and accountability is essential. Making evaluation reports and findings publicly available, ensuring public participation in the evaluation process, and establishing feedback and grievance redressal mechanisms can enhance transparency and build trust.

Achieving a balance between political undertakings and economic stability through monitoring and evaluation faces several challenges in the Indian context.

Let's explore some of them.

- There may be a need for more institutional capacity and expertise in monitoring and evaluation processes. Building a skilled workforce capable of conducting comprehensive evaluations and implementing robust monitoring systems is essential. Administration can address this by investing in training programs and creating specialized evaluation units within government agencies.

- Political pressures and short-term electoral cycles often prioritize rapid outcomes over long-term economic stability. This can hinder the objective assessment of policies and lead to the neglect of necessary adjustments or corrections. Balancing these competing interests requires a commitment to evidence-based decision-making and an understanding that short-term political gains must be aligned with Steady economic growth.

- Ensuring the independence and impartiality of monitoring and evaluation processes is crucial. Political interference or biases can undermine the credibility and objectivity of evaluations. Establishing independent evaluation bodies, involving external experts, and promoting straight-forwardness in the evaluation process can help mitigate these challenges.

- More financial, and technological resources may be needed to ensure the submission of robust M&E mechanisms.

- Investing in adequate infrastructure, information management systems, and data collection tools can enhance the efficiency and accuracy of monitoring and evaluation processes.

Monitoring and evaluation (M&E) mechanisms are critical for assessing the effectiveness and impact of multiple programs and initiatives. These mechanisms offer valuable insights into the progress, achievements, and areas of improvement, ensuring that resources are utilized efficiently and founding goals are effectively met.

However, there is often a need to strengthen M&E systems to enhance their reliability, accuracy, and relevance.

Let understand this from different angle now.

Political interference, biases, and conflicts of interest can compromise the integrity and credibility of M&E findings. Establishing independent evaluation units, fostering a culture of evaluation, and facilitating stakeholder engagement can mitigate these challenges.

- Firstly, integrating M&E into the project or program design phase is crucial. Clearly defining the objectives, outcomes, and indicators from the outset enables systematic monitoring throughout the evaluation process. Developing comprehensive monitoring and evaluation plans that outline data collection methods, frequency, and responsibilities is essential.

- Secondly, enhancing data collection and analysis capacities is vital. This includes developing standardized tools and methodologies, spreading the use of technology for data collection and management, and building the capacity of stakeholders in data analysis and interpretation. Incorporating innovative approaches such as mobile data collection, remote sensing, and data visualization can also improve the efficiency and accuracy of M&E processes.

- Thirdly, fostering partnerships and collaboration is essential. Engaging with academic institutions, research organizations, and civil society can bring diverse perspectives and expertise to monitoring and evaluation efforts. Partnerships can facilitate the exchange of knowledge, methodologies, and best practices, leading to improved M&E practices.

- Lastly, facilitating a learning culture and utilizing evaluation findings is crucial. Encouraging stakeholders to use M&E results for decision-making, incorporating feedback loops, and conducting regular evaluation-based reviews and reflections can drive continuous improvement in programs and policies.

Strengthening monitoring and evaluation mechanisms is essential for clear outcomes. By addressing challenges related to institutional capacity, resource constraints, independence, and objectivity, M&E systems can become robust, reliable, and relevant. The strategies of integrating M&E into project design, enhancing data collection and analysis capacities, fostering partnerships, and promoting a learning culture are crucial for strengthening M&E mechanisms.

With more robust monitoring and evaluation, established interventions can be more efficient, evidence-based, and accountable, leading to prolongable and impactful results.

Promoting Sustainable and Inclusive Development

Sustainable and broad-based development is a global priority in addressing social disparities, poverty and encouraging environmental stewardship. In this area, numerous social schemes and initiatives have been implemented worldwide.

Let us understand through some case studies that play a pivotal role in advancing Self-sustaining and general development through their objectives, strategies, and impact while emphasizing the importance of collaboration and collective action.

I. Universal Basic Income (UBI):

Universal Basic Income (UBI) is a social scheme that provides a regular, unconditional cash transfer to individuals, regardless of their income or employment status. It aims to reduce poverty, enhance social security, and promote inclusive development. UBI has gained traction globally as a potential solution to address income inequality and ensure all individuals have a basic standard of living.

Countries like Finland, Canada, and India have implemented pilot projects to assess the impact of UBI. By offering a safety net and empowering individuals to make choices that improve their well-being, UBI contributes to unceasing and comprehensive development.

II. National Health Insurance Schemes (NHIS):

National Health Insurance Schemes (NHIS) are social schemes that aim to provide affordable and accessible healthcare to all citizens. These schemes typically pool financial resources from individuals, employers, and the government to create a universal health coverage system.

NHIS promotes equitable access to healthcare services, reduces financial barriers, and enhances health outcomes. Examples include the National Health Insurance Scheme in Ghana and the National Health Service in the United Kingdom.

By prioritizing health as a fundamental right, NHIS contributes to inclusive expansion by ensuring that no one is left behind due to a lack of healthcare access.

III. Microfinance and Microcredit Programs:

Microfinance and microcredit programs grant small loans, savings, and financial services to low-income individuals and marginalized communities who lack access to traditional banking services. These programs aim to alleviate poverty, empower women, and foster entrepreneurship.

The Grameen Bank in Bangladesh, founded by Nobel Laureate Muhammad Yunus, is a prime example of the success of microfinance. By furnishing financial tools and training, microfinance and microcredit programs enable individuals to start businesses, generate income, and improve their standard of living. These schemes contribute to continual maturity by empowering individuals economically and fostering inclusive growth.

IV. Social Protection Programs:

Social protection programs encompass schemes such as conditional cash transfers, social pensions, and food assistance programs. These programs aim to provide a safety net for vulnerable populations, including children, older people, and impoverished individuals.

Successful Social protection programs have excellent outcomes like reducing poverty, improving nutrition, encouraging education, and breaking the cycle of intergenerational poverty.

By addressing social disparities and promoting human development, these schemes create an enabling environment for progress.

V. Education for All Initiatives:

Education for All initiatives strive to ensure access to quality education for all individuals, regardless of their socioeconomic background or geographical location. These initiatives prioritize fair education systems to eliminate gender disparities and produce lifelong learning opportunities.

The Global Partnership for Education and UNESCO's Education for All movement are driving forces behind these initiatives. By investing in education, these schemes empower individuals, enhance economic productivity, and foster social cohesion.

Education for all initiatives plays a critical role in viable forming by equipping individuals with the knowledge and skills needed to thrive in a rapidly changing world. Further, all-embracing development, which also plays a critical role here, requires concerted efforts and a multifaceted approach. Global social schemes such as Universal Basic Income, National Health Insurance Schemes, Microfinance and Microcredit Programs, Social Protection Programs, and Education for All Initiatives are critical drivers of change.

These schemes address social disparities, poverty, and lack of access to essential services. Their impact is evident in improved living standards, reduced inequality, enhanced health outcomes, and increased educational opportunities.

However, the success of these schemes relies on political commitment, functional implementation, and collaboration among governments, civil society organizations, and the private sector. By continuing to invest in social strategies and boosting their widespread adoption, we can pave the way for continuous and complete development on a global scale, ensuring a brighter future for all.

Collaborative Efforts for Effective Governance

Effective administration is crucial for addressing global challenges, endorsing development, and ensuring the correct decision-making in an increasingly interconnected and complex world. Traditional top-down approaches are supplemented by collaborative efforts that engage multiple stakeholders, including governments, civil society organizations, private sector entities, and citizens.

Collaborative governance or administration refers to the decision-making and problem-solving process involving diverse stakeholders working together to achieve shared goals. It recognizes the value of inclusivity, participation, and cooperation, fostering trust and mutual understanding among stakeholders. This approach moves beyond traditional hierarchical structures and encourages open dialogue, joint problem-solving, and collective action.

Benefits of Collaborative Governance:

Collaborative governance offers numerous advantages over traditional authority models.

- Firstly, it promotes inclusivity by ensuring diverse perspectives, interests, and voices are represented in decision-making processes. This leads to more neutral and informed outcomes that consider the needs of all stakeholders.

- Secondly, It enhances transparency and accountability, as multiple actors are involved in the decision-making process, reducing the risk of undue influence or corruption.

- Thirdly, it leverages the expertise and resources of different stakeholders, facilitating more comprehensive and reasoned solutions to complex challenges.

- Finally, it fosters ownership and buy-in from stakeholders, leading to increased implementation and sustainability of policies and initiatives.

Key Components of Collaborative Governance:

Impressive collaborative governance requires critical components that foster an environment of trust, cooperation, and shared responsibility. These components include:

- Inclusive participation: Encouraging the active involvement of all relevant stakeholders, ensuring that their perspectives and interests are heard and considered.

- Shared vision and goals: Establishing a common understanding of the desired outcomes and objectives, ensuring alignment and commitment from all stakeholders.

- Open and transparent communication: Promoting honest and timely information exchange, enabling stakeholders to make informed decisions and contribute effectively.

Collaborative decision-making processes: Employing consensus-building, negotiation, and mediation methods to facilitate joint decision-making and resolve conflicts.

- Resource sharing and capacity building: Pooling resources, expertise, and knowledge among stakeholders, strengthening their capacities to address complex issues.

- Adaptive and learning-oriented approach: Encouraging flexibility and continuous learning, adapting strategies based on feedback and evaluation, and incorporating lessons learned into future actions.

Successful Examples of Collaborative Governance:

Several successful examples demonstrate the effectiveness of collaborative regulation in achieving continued growth decision-making.

- Multi-Stakeholder Partnerships for Economic Resilience (MSPs): MSPs, such as the United Nations Global Compact and the Sustainable Development Solutions Network, bring together governments, businesses, civil society organizations, and academia to advance economic recovery goals. These partnerships leverage diverse stakeholders' expertise, resources, and networks to implement projects and initiatives at local, regional, and global levels.

- Participatory Budgeting: Participatory budgeting involves citizens in the decision-making process regarding the allocation of public funds. Cities like Porto Alegre in Brazil and Paris in France have successfully implemented participatory budgeting, giving residents a direct say in budget priorities and funding allocations. This approach fosters transparency, accountability, and citizen empowerment.

- Multi-Level Governance: Multi-level governance frameworks, such as the European Union, enable collaboration between national, regional, and local governments to address common challenges. These frameworks facilitate policy coordination, resource sharing, and knowledge exchange, leading to more efficient governance.

- Co-Management of Natural Resources: Collaborative approaches to managing natural resources, such as community-based conservation projects and co-management of forests and fisheries, have proven successful in ensuring continuous resource use. These initiatives involve the active engagement of local communities, indigenous groups, government agencies, and non-governmental organizations, leading to improved resource conservation and livelihoods.

- Social Impact Bonds (SIBs): SIBs are innovative financing mechanisms that bring together governments, private investors, and social service providers to address social issues. In SIBs, investors provide upfront funding for social programs, and the government repays them based on the program's success in achieving predetermined outcomes. This stakeholder collaboration ensures that funding is allocated efficiently, and products are completed.

Collaborative management empowers stakeholders by fostering inclusivity, transparency, and shared responsibility and leads to more informed, equitable, and persuasive decision-making. Successful examples from around the world demonstrate the ease of this approach, ranging from multi-stakeholder partnerships for the intensification of the economy to participatory budgeting and co-management of natural resources.

However, implementing collaborative Authority requires strong leadership, irresistible communication, and institutional support. Governments, civil society organizations, and other stakeholders must embrace this approach, invest in capacity building, and create enabling environments that facilitate collaboration. By harnessing the power of collaborative governance, we can drive favorable change, address global challenges, and build a worthwhile future for all.

Chapter Seven

Public Opinion and Citizen Awareness: Navigating the Impacts of Social Schemes

As per a publication by ET and written by Dr. R K Misha, "A social welfare scheme for its true success presupposes a reasonable clarity of the socio-economic need profile of the marginalized people, which will be the guiding anchor for specific welfare need to be addressed, and finally scheme-specific need to be covered penultimate objective."

In contemporary society, public opinion is no longer an abstract concept but a palpable force shaping policy and influencing outcomes. At the nexus of governance and public sentiment, we often find social schemes—policies designed to better societal well-being. These may range from healthcare plans to education initiatives or employment programs. While these schemes are well-intentioned, public opinion and citizen awareness invariably shape their real-world impact.

Public Opinion: The Invisible Hand that Steers Policy

The idea that the government should be "of the people, by the people, for the people" has always underscored the importance of public opinion in democratic societies. Governmental social schemes often stem from a perceived public need and are fueled by democratic consent. However, this relationship isn't unilateral. Public opinion can be a fickle companion. It can encourage and cripple social schemes depending on timing, framing, and the prevailing societal mood.

Citizen Awareness: The Keystone of Effective Social Schemes

While public opinion drives the social and political climate, citizen awareness is the keystone that can determine social schemes' ultimate success or failure. A well-informed citizenry is more likely to contribute constructively to policy formulation and implementation.

Importance of Information Dissemination

Governments need to employ multiple channels to disseminate accurate information about their schemes. Misinformation or lack of awareness can lead to reduced participation, stigmatization, or even failure of social programs. In developing countries, for example, many beneficial schemes often fall flat due to a need for more awareness among the intended beneficiaries.

The Role of Media

Media plays an indispensable role in shaping public opinion and awareness. Unfortunately, media outlets can sometimes focus on sensationalism over nuance, creating a distorted image of social schemes. Both traditional media (television, newspapers) and new media (social networks, blogs) have a role to play in educating the populace, and their power should not be underestimated. Government bodies must actively collaborate with media organizations to ensure accurate and widespread dissemination of information.

Navigating the Complex Interplay

Given the complexity and dynamism of public opinion and citizen awareness, how can governments navigate these waters effectively?

Transparency and Accountability

Being transparent about objectives, procedures, and limitations can go a long way in earning public trust. Government agencies must also be accountable for their actions and be willing to adapt schemes based on general feedback.

Public Consultation and Inclusion

Involving citizens in the decision-making process through public consultations or referendums can help tailor social schemes to meet general needs better and win citizen approval.

Education and Public Relations

Public relations campaigns that educate citizens on how they stand to benefit from social schemes can be highly effective. This not only boosts public opinion but also enhances citizen participation.

Monitoring and Feedback Mechanisms

Post-implementation, we must have robust monitoring and feedback mechanisms to assess social schemes' impact continually. This improves the system and provides data that can be used to sway public opinion positively.

Public opinion and citizen awareness about social schemes are essential factors that can influence the success or failure of these schemes. When people are aware of the benefits of social strategies and have a favorable opinion, they are more likely to participate in them. This can ensure that social schemes reach their intended beneficiaries and have a promising impact on society.

The governments of welfare states worldwide burn the significant midnight oil in rolling out social protection measures and schemes and spend considerable government revenue contributing to the same. The salient objective of the social protection schemes is to administer a reasonable level of support—be it in the form of food, health, or education, to families who are marginalized and can't afford a decent level of living.

The fact remains that often, a considerable number of people for whom the scheme in question is meant to stay excluded from the benefits. At the same time, some people do not need the help but end up receiving the benefits, thus causing benefit leakages.

In the wake of increasing social inequality and the need for objective opportunities, social schemes have become a prominent policy tool in many countries worldwide. These schemes address various societal challenges such as poverty, unemployment, healthcare, education, and social security. As a result, public opinion on social plans has gained significance, shaping policy decisions and political landscapes.

Ideological perspectives deeply influence public opinion on social schemes. We must explore the contrasting views of proponents who argue for the importance of social welfare and critics who emphasize individual responsibility and limited state intervention. By analyzing the arguments put forth by different ideological groups, we can gain insights into the diverse attitudes toward social schemes.

Public opinion and citizen awareness play a significant role in navigating the impacts of social schemes. Social schemes are designed to address societal issues and uplift vulnerable populations. Public opinion reflects citizens' perspectives, beliefs, and attitudes toward these schemes. Let's understand it better.

Firstly, Public opinion reflects citizens' needs, expectations, and satisfaction levels regarding social strategies. Policymakers and implementers can gather feedback and incorporate public opinion into these programs' design, implementation, and evaluation. This participatory approach enhances social schemes' responsiveness to the community's evolving needs.

It gives policymakers valuable insights into the public's perceptions and preferences, enabling them to make informed decisions and adapt policies to serve the community better.

Secondly, citizen awareness is crucial in ensuring the compelling utilization of social schemes. When citizens clearly understand these programs' purpose, benefits, and limitations, they are more likely to actively participate, engage with the initiatives, and utilize the available resources. Awareness empowers citizens to make informed choices, seek assistance when needed, and contribute to the success of the schemes.

Citizen awareness fosters active engagement and participation in the implementation process. Informed citizens are more likely to access the benefits and services provided by social schemes, ensuring that the intended beneficiaries receive the help they require. Citizen awareness also helps identify gaps and areas for improvement, enabling policymakers to address the challenges faced during implementation.

Furthermore, public opinion and citizen awareness contribute to accountability and transparency. When the public is aware of social schemes' objectives and expected outcomes, they become stakeholders in the process. They can hold policymakers and implementing agencies accountable to ensure resources are effectively utilized.

Public opinion and citizen awareness also act as mechanisms for quality control. Through feedback and public discourse, citizens can highlight issues, voice concerns, and suggest improvements. This input allows policymakers to make necessary adjustments and ensure that the social schemes are aligned with the expectations and realities on the ground.

The administration can develop strategies to push public opinion and citizen awareness in social schemes. Firstly, governments and implementing agencies should prioritize transparency and information dissemination.

Clear and accessible communication channels should be established to serve citizens with accurate and up-to-date information about social schemes' objectives, benefits, eligibility criteria, and application processes. This includes utilizing traditional media, social media platforms, community engagement, and public consultations.

These campaigns should focus on raising awareness about the existence of the programs, their purpose, and the rights and responsibilities of beneficiaries. Additionally, targeted efforts should be made to reach marginalized and vulnerable populations with limited access to information.

Furthermore, fostering civic engagement and citizen participation is crucial. Citizens should be encouraged to share feedback and experiences and actively contribute to designing and evaluating social schemes. Platforms such as public hearings, citizen advisory groups, and grievance redressal mechanisms can facilitate this engagement.

Public opinion and citizen awareness are instrumental in navigating the impacts of social schemes. By incorporating public opinion, policymakers can design more responsive programs that address the community's needs.

Citizen awareness empowers individuals to engage with these schemes actively, ensuring plausible utilization and enhancing outcomes. Promoting transparency, communication, education, and civic engagement are critical strategies for fostering public opinion and citizen awareness. By prioritizing these factors, governments can improve social schemes' accountability, transparency, and success, ultimately leading to greater social welfare and universal development.

Public opinion on social schemes is diverse and multifaceted, shaped by historical, ideological, and cultural factors.

While some countries demonstrate high levels of consensus, others experience significant debates and divisions.

Understanding public opinion is crucial for policymakers to design functional and renewable social schemes that meet the needs and aspirations of their citizens. By considering the global case studies and examining the challenges faced, policymakers can work towards addressing public concerns and building broad-based assistance for social schemes. Ultimately, through a nuanced understanding of public opinion, societies can strive toward more significant social equity and well-being.

As per an article published in worldbank.org on April 10, 2023, Citizens play a critical role in advocating and helping to make public institutions more transparent, accountable, and effective, and contributing innovative solutions to complex development challenges.

Growing evidence suggests that, under the right conditions, meaningful forms of citizen engagement and social accountability (CESA) can result in better governance, citizen empowerment, more positive and constructive citizen-state relations, strengthened public service delivery, and, ultimately, enhanced development effectiveness and well-being.

One of the good example of Citizens engagement is Smart City Mission India.

As per Nagrika.org, India's Smart city Mission (SCM) since its inception has focused on public participation using technology. It attempts to include citizen voices to build sustainable and inclusive cities. Cities are being encouraged to use systematic consultations with residents and stakeholders such that proposals and strategies come directly from the people.

Due to the specific focus on city development, urban mobility is one of the major themes of the program and the SCM has been one of the largest examples of facilitating citizen engagement in recent years. It has created a space for mass participation by augmenting ICT based tools, citizen consultation and cities are also using creative approaches like essay competitions, online polls, awareness campaigns and through social media. It continues to create experimental avenues for citizen engagement, such as the Streets for People challenge, Cycle for Change and a host of other initiatives that create space to seek opinions and inputs of common citizens.

Growing evidence suggests that, under the right conditions, meaningful forms of citizen engagement and social accountability (CESA) can result in better governance, citizen empowerment, more positive and constructive citizen-state relations, strengthened public service delivery, and, ultimately, enhanced development effectiveness and well-being.

Organized platforms for citizen engagement are just a few of the various spaces that are used for citizen engagement. News media is one of the oldest platforms that has been used by citizens to communicate with their local governments. Informal neighborhood groups and resident networks use news media to highlight local issues in maintenance and to voice their demands and concerns. Other modes like litigations and petitions have also been used, although not frequently, as bottom-up approaches to influence urban governance.

For example, in 2006, a coalition of resident welfare associations in Delhi went to court to defend their neighborhoods against what was seen as degrading informalization which led to the infamous Delhi Sealing Drive. Not very differently, Uber used its large consumer base to sign electronic petitions against Maharashtra City Taxi Rules that threatened the survival of the company.

However, the outcomes of citizen engagement are also context-specific and depend on the government and citizens' capacity and willingness to engage. Social, political, economic, environmental, cultural, geographic, and other factors, such as gender dynamics, shape the opportunities and scope for effective citizen engagement. Understanding the context in which CESA practices are undertaken and supporting enabling conditions are crucial to achieving results. This is particularly important in the current global context of shrinking civic space.

The study done by Nagrika.org says that small and medium sized cities have been able to engage more effectively through online mediums than metro cities. This indicated that civic intimacy between citizens and governments can be related to the scale of urban spread. The competitive approach of the smart city mission has also been a major factor for such cities to use aggressive approaches to enjoy more resources and opportunities. Better access to the internet and a larger population of youth and active age groups has a positive impact on participation. But increase in access to the internet did not necessarily lead to higher online participation in civic affairs, mainly as the medium is perceived for entertainment.

Social schemes are indispensable tools for societal improvement. However, their efficacy is heavily influenced by the ever-changing public opinion and citizen awareness. By understanding this intricate relationship, governments can implement more effective policies and create a more engaged and satisfied citizenry. Strategies such as transparent communication, public consultations, educational campaigns, and robust feedback mechanisms can significantly enhance the success of social schemes. Public opinion and citizen awareness are not just hurdles to overcome but valuable assets that can and should be harnessed for the common good.

As public participation emerges as a chance for citizens to voice their opinions in decision making, planning processes are also becoming responsive to this change. There is a need to bridge the gap between 'invited' and 'created' spaces of citizen engagement through more collaborations between the government and community-based organizations.

Chapter Eight

Global Case Studies: Assessing the Impact of Pre-Election Social Schemes

To truly assess the impact of pre-election social schemes, it's crucial to evaluate their effectiveness and longevity. Are they adequately reaching the intended beneficiaries? Are there checks and balances to prevent corruption and misuse? Most importantly, do these schemes have a life beyond the electoral cycle, or do they fade away once the ballots have been counted?

Assessing the impact of pre-election social schemes on electoral outcomes is a critical aspect of political science. Here are some top global case studies that demonstrate how these schemes might influence voting behavior.

United States: Tax Cuts and Stimulus Checks

- **Scheme**: In the year leading up to a Presidential election, the incumbent administration announces sweeping tax cuts and sends out stimulus checks to citizens.

- **Short-term Impact**: Increase in consumer spending, boost in stock market, and positive sentiment among voters.

- **Long-term Impact**: Budget deficits increase, future administrations are left with less fiscal room for implementing new policies.

- **Assessment**: While the scheme boosts the incumbent's

popularity in the short term, it places a long-term strain on public finances and may limit future investment in areas such as education, healthcare, and infrastructure.

India: Free Electricity for Farmers

- Scheme: Free electricity for irrigation.
- Short-term impact: Lowered costs for farmers, increased agricultural output.
- Long-term impact: Strain on electrical grid, fiscal deficit.
- Assessment: Short-term gains but long-term sustainability concerns

Brazil: Bolsa Família Expansion

- **Scheme:** An expansion of the existing Bolsa Família program is announced, increasing the cash payments to low-income families ahead of the election.
- **Short-term Impact:** Improves living conditions for beneficiaries and boosts popularity of the ruling party among low-income demographics.
- **Long-term Impact:** Could contribute to reduced poverty and better social mobility if well-managed, but also has the potential to create dependency if not coupled with other forms of social advancement.
- **Assessment**: The expanded scheme can have both positive and negative outcomes. Proper management and planning are essential to ensure long-term benefits.

India: Farm Loan Waivers

- **Scheme:** Ahead of state and national elections, governments often announce farm loan waivers to attract the large voter base of farmers.

- **Short-term Impact:** Alleviates financial stress among farmers, boosts incumbent popularity among rural communities.

- **Long-term Impact:** Causes fiscal imbalances, increases moral hazard, and doesn't address structural issues plaguing agriculture.

- **Assessment:** The measure is often effective in winning elections but fails to provide a sustainable solution to agricultural issues. It also undermines the credit culture, affecting financial institutions in the long run.

Brazil: Police Surge in Crime-Hotspots

- **Scheme:** Increased police presence in high-crime areas.

- **Short-term Impact:** Lower crime rates, increased safety perception.

- **Long-term Impact:** Potential civil rights concerns, budgetary strain.

- **Assessment:** Effective but contentious

United Kingdom: NHS Funding Boost

- **Scheme:** Increased funding for the National Health Service (NHS) announced ahead of general elections.

- **Short-term Impact:** Public sentiment improves due to better healthcare services, increased trust in the incumbent government.

- **Long-term Impact:** Unless the funding is sustainable, it could lead to financial strain in subsequent years.

- **Assessment:** Such a scheme generally wins public approval but needs to be financially sustainable and well-executed to ensure that it does not result in future cutbacks or deficits.

Germany: Renewable Energy Incentives

- **Scheme:** Subsidies for renewable energy technology adoption.
- **Short-term Impact:** Increased adoption rates, reduced carbon emissions.
- **Long-term Impact:** Market distortion if not executed properly.
- **Assessment:** Environmentally beneficial but needs long-term planning

United Kingdom: Pension Increases

- **Scheme:** Boosting pension payouts.
- **Short-term Impact:** Boost to senior citizen welfare and happiness.
- **Long-term Impact:** Demographic changes make this financially unsustainable.
- **Assessment:** Popular but financially risky.

South Africa: Free Higher Education Announcement

- **Scheme:** Free higher education is announced for students from low-income families before the general elections.
- **Short-term Impact:** Increased enrollment rates, positive public sentiment.
- **Long-term Impact:** Strain on national budget, potential devaluation of tertiary education if not properly managed.
- **Assessment:** While the scheme is politically popular and has noble goals, it requires careful financial planning and academic structure to be sustainable and effective in the long term.

Australia: Childcare Subsidies

- **Scheme:** Increased subsidies for childcare services.
- **Short-term Impact:** Boost to workforce participation rates, particularly among women.
- **Long-term Impact:** Risk of inflating childcare costs.
- **Assessment:** Generally positive if managed correctly

Japan: Youth Employment Programs

- **Scheme:** Government-funded internships and training for youth.
- **Short-term Impact:** Lower youth unemployment rates.
- **Long-term Impact:** Skills may not match market demand.
- **Assessment:** Mixed outcomes, dependent on implementation.

Canada: Housing Grants for First-Time Buyers

- **Scheme:** Financial incentives for first-time homebuyers.
- **Short-term Impact:** Stimulated housing market, increased ownership.
- **Long-term Impact:** Potential housing bubble.
- **Assessment:** Risky but popular.

Mexico: Small Business Loans

- **Scheme:** Low-interest loans for small businesses.
- **Short-term Impact:** Boost to local economies, job creation.
- **Long-term Impact:** Default risk and fiscal pressure.
- **Assessment:** Requires strong financial oversight.

South Africa: Free Public Transport

- **Scheme:** Free public transportation for all citizens.
- **Short-term Impact:** Increased mobility, reduced expenses for lower-income groups.
- **Long-term Impact:** Strain on public infrastructure.
- **Assessment:** Financially challenging but socially impactful.

United States: Universal Healthcare Pilot

- **Scheme:** A one-year pilot of universal healthcare is implemented in a few states as a prelude to a national rollout.
- **Short-term Impact:**
  - Public Opinion: Surveys show a significant uptick in approval ratings for the incumbent administration.
  - Healthcare Access: Millions of uninsured or underinsured individuals gain access to healthcare services.
- **Long-term Impact:**
  - Financial Strain: Concerns about the scheme's sustainability surface as it contributes to an increase in the federal deficit.
  - Healthcare Quality: There's a debate about potential degradation in healthcare quality due to overburdened services.
- **Assessment:** The scheme proves to be popular in the short term and could theoretically lead to healthier citizens over time. However, questions around long-term funding and quality control are significant concerns that future administrations will need to address.

France: Free Healthcare for Children

- Scheme: Expanded free healthcare services for children.
- Short-term impact: Increased wellness among children, relieved parental burden.
- Long-term impact: Strain on healthcare budget.
- Assessment: Socially beneficial but financially taxing.

Germany: Tuition-Free Higher Education

- **Scheme:** Abolishment of tuition fees for higher education, funded by federal subsidies.
- **Short-term Impact:**
    - Enrollment Rates: Higher enrollment rates, particularly among low-income households.
    - Public Opinion: Youth voter turnout increases, favoring the incumbent government.
- **Long-term Impact:**
    - Financial Strain: Sustainability concerns arise due to increased government spending.
    - Academic Standards: Concerns grow about the potential for degradation of academic standards due to overcrowded institutions.
- **Assessment:** The scheme succeeds in making higher education accessible but raises important questions about quality and financial sustainability.

Japan: Elderly Care Grants

- **Scheme:** The government provides significant grants to municipalities to expand elderly care services.
- **Short-term Impact:**

- o Elderly Welfare: Immediate improvements in the quality of elderly care services.
- o Public Opinion: Elderly population and their families express strong approval, benefiting the incumbent party.

- **Long-term Impact:**
  - o Demographic Shift: Given Japan's aging population, the scheme is likely to face financial sustainability issues in the long run.
  - o Healthcare Budget: May impact budget allocations for other essential healthcare services.

- **Assessment:** While the scheme has strong electoral benefits and improves elderly care, long-term financial sustainability remains a challenge.

Brazil: Land Redistribution Program

- **Scheme:** The government promises and initiates the redistribution of land to indigenous communities and landless farmers.

- **Short-term Impact:**
  - o Community Welfare: Immediate benefits to marginalized communities through land ownership.
  - o Public Opinion: Popular among lower-income demographics, although it causes political polarization.

- **Long-term Impact:** Economic Development: Questions arise regarding how the redistributed lands will be developed sustainably.
  - o Property Rights: Conflicts related to land and property rights emerge, creating social tension.

- **Assessment:** The scheme addresses a critical social issue and has immediate electoral benefits but opens complex legal and economic challenges that may take years to resolve

Kenya's Harambee Initiatives

- **Background:** "Harambee" is a Swahili word for "pulling together." Over the years, many politicians in Kenya initiated community development projects under this banner before elections.

- **Impact:** These initiatives, though meant for community development, have sometimes been viewed as a means to gain electoral favor, with politicians using them to showcase their dedication to community welfare.

Turkey's Coal Distributions

- **Background:** In the run-up to elections, there were instances where Turkish politicians distributed coal and other basic goods to low-income households.

- **Impact:** Such distributions, although short-term relief measures, were criticized as efforts to attract votes.

Indonesia's Pilkada (Direct Local Elections) and Social Assistance Program

- **Background:** After 2005, Indonesia saw a rise in direct local leader elections. Around the same time, various social assistance programs like fuel subsidies and cash transfers were rolled out.

- **Impact:** Researchers found a significant relationship between the disbursal of social assistance and increased vote shares for incumbents in the subsequent elections.

Brazil's Bolsa Família

- **Background**: Launched in 2003, Bolsa Família is a social welfare program aiming to provide financial aid to poor Brazilian families.

- **Impact**: Studies have shown a positive correlation between the program's expansion and increased support for the ruling party during election periods. It is seen as a cornerstone of Brazil's welfare initiatives.

Mexico's Progresa/Oportunidades/Prospera Program

- **Background**: Initiated in 1997, this conditional cash transfer program provides money to poor households when they meet certain conditions like school attendance and health check-ups.

- **Impact**: The program was associated with increased support for the incumbent party, although its impact on voting patterns is debated.

United States' Election Year Fiscal Policy

- **Background**: Historically, the US has seen various fiscal stimuli and social programs rolled out during election years.

- **Impact**: While not always directly tied to elections, studies suggest that economic policy can be influenced by electoral cycles, with governments often increasing spending or providing tax cuts in election years.

Ghana's Pre-election Electricity Provision

- **Background**: Prior to elections, there has been a noticeable effort by governments in Ghana to improve electricity provision.

- **Impact**: Such efforts, especially when they result in noticeable infrastructure development, tend to garner support for the ruling party, showcasing the direct influence of public utility provisions on electoral gains.

Each of these case studies demonstrates the immediate and potential long-term impacts of pre-election social schemes. These policies often have multifaceted consequences that can shape public opinion, influence election outcomes, and have lasting implications for governance and financial stability.

Chapter Nine

Evaluating the Effectiveness and Efficiency of Pre-Election Social Schemes

Pre-election social schemes are government programs that provide citizens with social benefits and welfare measures in the run-up to elections. These schemes are often implemented to garner political influence towards voters. However, evaluating these schemes' effectiveness and efficiency is essential to ensure they genuinely address societal needs and deliver promising outcomes.

Evaluating pre-election social schemes is crucial for several reasons.

Firstly, it ensures accountability and transparency in the use of public funds. By assessing, governments can determine whether the allocated resources are utilized effectively and efficiently to achieve the desired outcomes. This helps prevent the misuse of funds for political gains and promotes responsible governance.

Secondly, evaluation allows for evidence-based decision-making. Through rigorous assessment, policymakers can assess the impact of pre-election social schemes on the target population and make informed choices regarding program continuation, modification, or termination. It enables policymakers to allocate resources based on the actual priorities of the people rather than mere political expediency.

Furthermore, evaluation enhances the overall effectiveness and efficiency of social schemes. By identifying strengths and weaknesses, evaluations provide insights into the program's design, implementation, and delivery mechanisms. This information can be utilized to make necessary improvements, streamline processes, and enhance the overall impact on the intended beneficiaries.

Evaluating pre-election social schemes poses several challenges.

- There may be inherent biases in the evaluation process, as the very nature of these schemes is politically driven. The risk of manipulation and skewed reporting exists, as stakeholders may be motivated to present hopeful results to influence the electoral outcome. This challenge necessitates the establishment of independent evaluation mechanisms and the involvement of external experts to ensure objectivity.

- Time constraints pose a challenge in conducting comprehensive evaluations. Pre-election social schemes are often implemented within a limited timeframe, leaving insufficient time for a thorough assessment of their impact. This time constraint requires careful planning and allocation of resources to conduct evaluations within the available timeframe effectively.

- Accessing reliable and accurate data can be challenging. Transparency and data availability are critical for meaningful evaluations. However, political considerations may lead to limited data transparency or data manipulation for political gains. Overcoming this challenge requires robust data collection and management systems and ensuring data integrity and independence in data analysis.

To effectively evaluate pre-election social schemes, the administration can adopt several strategies like–

- Establishing an independent evaluation body is essential to ensure objectivity and credibility. This body should be separate from political influence and vested interests, allowing for impartial assessments of scheme effectiveness and efficiency.

- Employing rigorous evaluation methodologies is crucial. Utilizing mixed method approaches that combine quantitative and qualitative data collection techniques can impart a comprehensive understanding of the scheme's impact. Surveys, interviews, focus group discussions, and case studies can be used to gather data from beneficiaries, program implementers, and other relevant stakeholders.

- Ensuring transparency and data accessibility is vital. Evaluation reports should be made publicly available to boost transparency and liability. Additionally, efforts should be made to establish reliable and independent data sources to avoid any manipulation or biases in data collection and analysis.

Stakeholder engagement and participation should be encouraged throughout the evaluation process. This includes involving beneficiaries, civil society organizations, and experts in evaluating the schemes' impact and efficiency. Their inputs and perspectives can enrich the evaluation findings and provide a more comprehensive understanding of the scheme's outcomes.

Evaluating pre-election social schemes is essential to ensure accountability, transparency, and credible utilization of public resources. Overcoming challenges such as biases, time constraints, and data reliability requires independent evaluation mechanisms, rigorous methodologies, and transparent data practices.

Governments can accurately assess the effectiveness and efficiency of pre-election social schemes by implementing strategies that promote objectivity, data integrity, and stakeholder engagement. This evaluation process enables evidence-based decision-making, enhances program impact, and strengthens democratic leadership by aligning social projects with the genuine necessities and priorities of the population.

Let's understand this through other factors.

Successes and Positive Outcomes

Despite their political nature, pre-election social schemes can bring successes and conclusive aftermath in certain circumstances. While it is essential to approach these schemes with a critical lens, it is also necessary to acknowledge their potential benefits. Here are some of the successes and helpful conclusions that pre-election social strategies can achieve:

- Addressing Immediate Social Needs
- Increased Access to Services
- Empowerment and Social Inclusion
- Public Awareness and Engagement
- Political Accountability
- Definite Impact on Social Indicators

Independent evaluation mechanisms and transparent reporting are necessary to ensure these outgrowths are not distorted or exaggerated for political gains. Additionally, The administration should carefully monitor these schemes' long-term sustainability and effectiveness beyond the electoral cycle to ensure continued categorial or assured impacts on society.

Unintended Consequences

Social schemes in India are designed to uplift marginalized sections of society. While many of these initiatives have shown promise, there have also been instances of unintended consequences.

It is essential to be aware of the unintended consequences of pre-election social schemes so that we can mitigate them and maximize their benefits. We need to find ways to ensure that these schemes are sustainable, do not create a culture of dependency, and are not subject to corruption. We also need to be mindful of the environmental impacts of pre-election social schemes.

In India, pre-election social schemes have become increasingly common in recent years. This is due to several factors, including:

- The growing importance of elections: Elections in India are becoming increasingly competitive, and leaders are looking for ways to gain an edge over their opponents.

- The increasing poverty and inequality in India: Many Indians are struggling to make ends meet and are more likely to vote for lawmakers who promise to help them.

- The rise of populism: Populist politicians often promise to provide generous social welfare benefits and have successfully won elections in India.

By carefully considering the unintended consequences of pre-election social schemes, we can ensure that they are used to improve the lives of millions of Indians without creating new problems.

Here are some additional unintended consequences of pre-election social schemes in India:

- **Decreased Accountability:** In some cases, when statemen are seen as buying votes with social schemes, it can lead to reduced responsibility. This is because voters may feel they do not need to hold politicians accountable for their promises, as they can always be bought off with more handouts.

- **Increased Polarization:** Pre-election social schemes can sometimes be used to divide voters along social or religious lines. This is because politicians may target specific voters with promises of benefits to win their support.

- **Discouraged Investment:** When the government is seen as being unreliable or corrupt, it can discourage investment. This is because businesses may be reluctant to invest in a country where they are unsure if their assets will be protected.

It is essential to be aware of these consequences so that we can mitigate them and maximize the benefits of these schemes. We need to find ways to ensure that pre-election social schemes are sustainable and do not create a culture of dependency.

Let's explore a couple of schemes through examples from India & US:

1. United States' Supplemental Nutrition Assistance Program (SNAP): SNAP, formerly known as Food Stamps, is a federal program that provides food assistance to low-income individuals and families. The program has been credited with reducing hunger and malnutrition in the United States. However, it has also been criticized for being abused and subject to fraud.

2. Public Distribution System (PDS)

The Public Distribution System (PDS) is a subsidized food distribution program implemented by the Indian government. However, it has been plagued by numerous challenges, leading to significant failures. One of the main issues is corruption, where food grains meant for people experiencing poverty are siphoned off by corrupt officials and intermediaries.

This deprives the intended beneficiaries and perpetuates the cycle of poverty. Additionally, many other issues, like inefficiencies in storage, transportation, and distribution, have resulted in food grain rotting or reaching the market at higher prices, further undermining the program's effectiveness.

3. Mahatma Gandhi National Rural Employment Guarantee Act (MGNREGA):

The MGNREGA was introduced to provide employment opportunities and ensure livelihood security in rural areas. While it has generated employment for many, there have been unintended consequences.

The scheme often fails to create productive assets, focusing more on manual labor than skill development. This has led to the perpetuation of low-skill jobs, limiting the long-term impact on poverty alleviation.

Furthermore, instances of corruption and mismanagement have been reported, undermining the transparency and efficiency of the program.

4. Midday Meal Scheme:

The Midday Meal Scheme aims to provide nutritious meals to school children, with the dual objective of reducing malnutrition and promoting school attendance. However, several unintended consequences have emerged. In some cases, poor quality or contaminated food has resulted in health issues among children. Moreover, the scheme has inadvertently led to a decline in the quality of education, as the focus often shifts to providing meals rather than improving teaching and learning outcomes.

5. Aadhaar System:

The Aadhaar system, a biometric identification program, was introduced to improve the efficiency and transparency of social welfare schemes. However, concerns have been raised regarding privacy violations. Aadhaar-related fraud and identity theft have emerged, compromising trust in the system. Additionally, the exclusion of eligible beneficiaries due to technological glitches or discrepancies in data has led to the denial of benefits to those who need them the most.

6. Swachh Bharat Mission (Clean India Mission):

The Swachh Bharat Mission aimed to achieve universal sanitation coverage and eliminate open defecation. While the program witnessed considerable success constructing toilets and creating awareness, the sustainability and behavioral change aspects have proven challenging. In some areas, newly constructed toilets still need to be cleaned or maintained adequately due to cultural or traditional practices, inadequate water supply, or lack of proper sanitation infrastructure.

In addition to the examples mentioned above, here are some other unintended consequences of pre-election social schemes that have been observed in the last three years:

- **Increased Inflation:** When pre-election social schemes are implemented without careful planning, they can lead to inflation. This is because they can increase the money supply, increasing prices.

- **Increased Debt:** When pre-election social schemes are funded by borrowing, they can lead to increased debt. This can make it difficult for the government to finance other essential services in the future.

- **Disruption of Markets:** When pre-election social schemes distort markets, they can lead to disorder. This is because they can make it difficult for businesses to plan and invest.

This highlights the importance of a holistic approach, encompassing behavioral change campaigns and long-term maintenance strategies. While social schemes in India have made significant strides in addressing failures and unintended consequences, they have been encountered along the way.

Corruption, mismanagement, inadequate infrastructure, and

behavioral factors have contributed to the underperformance of specific initiatives. Identifying and rectifying these issues is crucial to ensure social schemes' competent implementation and long-term success. Transparency, accountability, and active participation of all stakeholders are vital to mitigating failures and unintended consequences, ultimately leading to more impactful social development in India.

Social Impact Assessment and Monitoring Mechanisms for Social Schemes

Social schemes are an integral part of any welfare-oriented government. These schemes aim to uplift marginalized segments of society and ensure total reformation. However, it is crucial to assess and monitor the social impact of these schemes to ensure their effectiveness, accountability, and supportable outcomes.

Let's explore the significance of social impact assessment (SIA) and monitoring mechanisms for social schemes, highlighting their components and their role in enhancing the impact of such initiatives.

Social Impact Assessment (SIA) for Social Schemes:

Social Impact Assessment is a systematic process that helps evaluate the potential social consequences of implementing a social scheme. It involves studying and analyzing the likely impacts on various aspects, including livelihoods, health, education, gender equality, and community dynamics. SIA ensures that the scheme's design and implementation consider the concerns of the target beneficiaries and affected communities.

Critical components of SIA for social schemes include:

- **Stakeholder Engagement:** Engaging with relevant stakeholders, such as community representatives, civil society organizations, and local government officials, is crucial in understanding their perspectives, needs, and aspirations. Involving them in the decision-making process helps ensure inclusivity and ownership of the social scheme.

- **Baseline Assessment:** This involves gathering data and information about the target area's existing social, economic, and cultural conditions. It helps to establish a benchmark against which the impact of the social scheme can be measured.

- **Impact Identification and Assessment**: This step involves identifying the social scheme's potential constructive and obstructive impacts on different social aspects. It assesses these impacts' magnitude, duration, and distribution to determine the scheme's social footprint.

- **Mitigation Measures:** SIA recommends specific mitigation measures to minimize adverse social impacts and enhance useful ones. These measures may include capacity building, skill development, social infrastructure development, and community participation strategies.

Enhancing Effectiveness and Accountability:

The incorporation of social impact assessment and monitoring mechanisms within social schemes enhances their overall effectiveness and accountability in several ways:

- **Evidence-Based Decision Making:** SIA provides a scientific basis for decision-making, ensuring that the design and implementation of social schemes are rooted in empirical data and analysis. Monitoring mechanisms then offer ongoing feedback to assess the scheme's progress and make necessary adjustments, enhancing its impact over time.

- **Stakeholder Participation and Ownership:** Involving stakeholders in the assessment and monitoring processes fosters a sense of ownership and empowerment. It ensures that the voices of the affected circles are heard, leading to contextually relevant social schemes.

- **Early Detection of Issues and Mitigation:** Monitoring mechanisms help identify potential issues or challenges in implementing social schemes at an early stage. This allows for timely intervention and the implementation of mitigation measures, reducing the negative impacts and improving overall outcomes.

- **Transparency and Accountability:** Social impact assessment and monitoring mechanisms provide a transparent framework for evaluating the effectiveness and accountability of social schemes. They enable stakeholders to hold implementing agencies and policymakers accountable for the intended effects and ensure that resources are utilized optimally.

Monitoring Mechanisms for Social Schemes

Monitoring mechanisms play a crucial role in tracking the progress and evaluating the social impact of implemented social schemes. They provide valuable insights into the scheme's effectiveness, identify deviations from intended outcomes, and help inform decision-making processes. Critical components of monitoring mechanisms for social methods include:

- **Performance Indicators:** Defining clear and measurable indicators is essential for monitoring the progress and impact of social schemes. These indicators can include parameters such as employment generation, poverty reduction, access to critical services, and social indicators like education and health improvements.

- **Data Collection and Analysis:** Regular data collection and analysis related to the social scheme's implementation and follow-ups are necessary. This can involve quantitative and qualitative methods to understand the scheme's impact on social aspects comprehensively.

- **Stakeholder Feedback:** Seeking feedback from beneficiaries, implementing agencies, and other stakeholders helps understand their experiences and perspectives regarding the social scheme. This feedback provides valuable insights and can help identify areas for improvement or course correction.

- **Evaluation and Reporting:** Periodic evaluation of the social scheme's performance against predefined indicators helps assess its effectiveness. The findings should be documented and reported transparently to stakeholders, policymakers, and the public, ensuring accountability and enabling evidence-based decision-making.

Social impact assessment and monitoring mechanisms are essential to social schemes, ensuring their effectiveness, accountability, and sustainability. Through comprehensive assessment, stakeholder engagement, and ongoing monitoring, these mechanisms facilitate evidence-based decision-making, early issue detection, and course correction.

By incorporating these tools, social schemes can achieve their objectives & promote unrestricted and vast development. It is imperative for governments, policymakers, and implementing agencies to prioritize social impact assessment and monitoring mechanisms to maximize the unequivocal social impact of their welfare initiatives.

Pre-election social schemes have become a common practice in many countries, aiming to garner support and secure votes from the electorate. These schemes, although well-intentioned, often need help with transparency, accountability, and the sustainability of their impact.

Policymakers must consider key policy recommendations to ensure pre-election social schemes' compelling implementation and long-term benefits. Clear and transparent eligibility criteria should be established to avoid potential favoritism and misuse of pre-election social plans. These criteria should be based on objective measures such as income levels, socio-economic indicators, or specific demographic groups.

Additionally, the selection process should be transparent, ensuring beneficiaries are selected solely based on their eligibility and without political bias or influence. Establishing independent oversight and monitoring mechanisms is crucial to ensure transparency, accountability, and the proper implementation of pre-election social schemes.

These mechanisms can include independent monitoring committees, civil society organizations, or auditing bodies responsible for monitoring the entire process, from scheme design to implementation and evaluation. Regular audits, evaluations, and public reporting of the scheme's progress will help to maintain integrity and public trust.

Pre-election social schemes should not be limited to short-term benefits aimed at electoral gains. A comprehensive impact assessment framework should be implemented to evaluate the long-term effects of these schemes on the intended beneficiaries and society as a whole.

This assessment should measure the sustainability of the scheme's impact, including its contribution to poverty reduction, improved access to essential services, and long-term social development. Based on the impact assessment, policymakers can design sustainability plans to ensure the continuation and effectiveness of the scheme beyond the election cycle.

Strengthening existing social welfare institutions is crucial to ensure the righteous and reasonable delivery of pre-election social schemes. This includes investing in capacity building for government agencies responsible for scheme implementation, improving their technical expertise, and enhancing their administrative capabilities.

Transparent communication and public awareness campaigns are essential to inform citizens about pre-election social schemes' objectives, eligibility criteria, and benefits.

This will empower citizens to participate actively, hold policymakers accountable, and report any irregularities or exclusions. Engaging civil society organizations, media outlets, and community leaders can help disseminate accurate information and facilitate public scrutiny of the schemes.

Pre-election social schemes should operate within a robust legal and ethical framework. Clear guidelines should be established to prevent the misuse of public resources for electoral gains. Anti-corruption measures and strict enforcement of ethical standards should be implemented to deter any form of bribery, coercion, or vote-buying associated with these schemes.

Political parties and candidates should adhere to a code of conduct that ensures fair and transparent implementation. Pre-election social schemes can serve as decisive social welfare and development tools if designed, implemented, and monitored effectively.

The policy for the betterment of society must include transparent selection processes, independent oversight, long-term impact assessment, strengthening social welfare institutions, public awareness, and ethical enforcement, which can enhance the transparency, accountability, and impact of such schemes.

By implementing these recommendations, policymakers can ensure that pre-election social schemes genuinely benefit the intended beneficiaries and contribute to sustainable social development while promoting public trust in the electoral process.

Chapter Ten

Ethical Considerations: Balancing Political Ambitions and Public Welfare

Political leaders often find themselves at a crossroads where their ambitions and public welfare converge. The ethical dilemma of balancing these two interests has been a subject of great concern and debate for years. In democratic societies where elections are an intrinsic part of governance, politicians frequently resort to pre-election social schemes to secure votes.

While some of these schemes may align with public welfare and contribute to long-term betterment, others can be short-sighted, poorly implemented, or driven purely by the motive to win elections.

The Nature of the Dilemma

Politicians' survival depends on votes, maintaining public support, and securing their position in the ever-volatile public opinion landscape. On the other hand, the public looks to politicians to improve their social, economic, and general welfare.

Here lies the crux of the ethical dilemma: Should politicians prioritize their political survival or focus solely on long-term, sustainable projects that may yield only some immediate electoral benefits?

On the one hand, political leaders have a responsibility to their constituents to act in their best interests. This means making decisions that will benefit the majority of people, even if those decisions do not satisfy the political leader personally. On the other hand, political leaders are also individuals with their dreams and goals. They may want to achieve power or prestige. This can sometimes lead them to make decisions that are not in the public's best interests but benefit them in other ways.

Let see the factors that can influence how political leaders balance their personal ambition and public welfare i.e.

- **The Political System is in Place:** In some scenarios, such as a dictatorship, political leaders have much more power and discretion than in others, such as a democracy. This can make it easier for political leaders in dictatorships to pursue their ambitions, even at the expense of the public welfare.

- **The Society's Culture**: An organization's values and norms can also influence how political leaders behave. For example, in communities where corruption is widespread, political leaders may be more likely to put their interests ahead of the public good.

- **The Individual Political Leader's Character and Values:** Ultimately, deciding whether to put personal ambition ahead of public welfare is unique for each political leader. Some leaders are more driven by self-interest than others, and some are more committed to serving the public good.

Short-Term Gain vs. Long-Term Benefit

Initiatives like tax cuts, subsidies, and welfare schemes can often bring immediate relief or benefits to the electorate. However, they may also lead to budgetary imbalances and economic instability and undermine long-term policy planning. When politicians opt for schemes that offer immediate rewards but lack long-term vision, they engage in ethical compromise. They may win the election but fail to act in the best interests of the public they represent, sacrificing long-term welfare for short-term political gains.

The Importance of Civic Engagement

Finally, the public also has a role in ensuring that political leaders act in their best interests. Citizens can hold their elected officials accountable by voting for candidates representing their interests. They can also participate in civic activities, such as protests and demonstrations, to make their voices heard. When citizens are engaged in the political process, it is more difficult for political leaders to make decisions that are not in the public's best interests.

Let's explore the Ethical Frameworks for Consideration through some of the concepts below.

- **Consequentialism:** From a consequentialist perspective, an action is deemed ethical if it results in the most favorable outcome for the most significant number of people. Under this framework, pre-election schemes could be justified if they serve the greater good. However, the greater good is not just a measure of immediate impact but should also account for long-term sustainability and overall societal progress.

- **Deontological Ethics**: Deontological ethics would assess the ethicality of an action based on the activity itself rather than its outcomes. In this framework, sacrificing long-term public welfare for short-term political gain would be inherently unethical, irrespective of whether it wins votes.

- **Virtue Ethics:** In virtue ethics, the focus shifts to the character of the individual making the decision. A virtuous politician would be guided by qualities like integrity, wisdom, and a genuine concern for public welfare, even when making decisions that could impact their political career negatively.

Let's also understand through a case study: The Affordable Care Act in the United States In the U.S., the Affordable Care Act or 'Obamacare' was a controversial move aimed at public health's long-term betterment. Politically, it was a double-edged sword, garnering both praise and criticism. Ethically speaking, the initiative seemed to align more closely with the long-term welfare of the public despite the political risks involved.

Let's move further.

While managing public welfare, governments must accelerate economic development through their decisions on public expenditures. Public expenditures, allocated appropriately, can overcome market failures that exacerbate poverty, such as the inability of poor people to borrow for education or to learn about preventive health care or the existence of externalities that increase the public health hazards that disproportionately hurt poor people. Allocation is often inappropriate, however.

Public spending goes to wage bills for bulky state administrations, farm subsidies absorbed by the wealthiest farmers, or public works projects with limited public utility, all at the expense of the quality of public services. Many efforts worldwide to "empower" poor people, whether through devolved decision-making or participatory budgeting, are all responses to any failures of government expenditure policies.

Balancing political ambitions and public welfare requires ethical considerations to guide decision-making and encourage accountability, transparency, and comprehensive governance.

Upholding integrity, ensuring accountability to the public, practicing transparency, embracing complete decision-making processes, avoiding conflicts of interest, conducting ethical campaigns, and prioritizing long-term sustainability are essential elements in striking this delicate balance.

In a democracy, the public elects representatives to act in their best interests. These representatives are entrusted with the power to make decisions that will impact the lives of their constituents. However, there is always the potential for these representatives, and some of them sometimes put their political ambitions ahead of the public welfare, too.

This is a complex issue with no easy answers.

Many factors can influence a political decision-making process, including personal beliefs, the party's platform, and the pressure of special interests. It is essential to consider all these factors when evaluating whether a politician is acting in the public's best interests. Political leaders must recognize that their ambitions can only be significant when they serve the public's best interests, safeguarding citizens' rights and well-being.

By upholding ethical principles, leaders can build trust, design social cohesion, and advance the common good, ensuring that political ambitions are grounded in moral Regulation and genuine commitment to public welfare.

There are several ethical considerations that many politicians should keep in mind when balancing their political ambitions with public welfare.

- First, they should always be honest and transparent with their constituents. They should not make promises they cannot keep and should not mislead the public about their intentions.

- Second, many politicians should be answerable or accountable to their constituents. They should listen to the concerns of the people they represent and be willing to change their positions if they are convinced that the public is correct.

- Third, many politicians should be willing to put the interests of the public ahead of their interests. This may mean making unpopular decisions with their party or special interests. However, many politicians must remember that they are elected to serve the people, not themselves.

In politics, leaders are often driven by their ambitions to secure power and advance their agendas. While political ambition is an inherent aspect of the democratic process, it must be balanced with a genuine commitment to public welfare. Ethical considerations play a crucial role in ensuring that political ambitions do not compromise the well-being and rights of the public.

Let's understand the ethical dilemmas that arise when balancing political ambitions and public welfare, highlighting the importance of integrity, accountability, transparency, and integrative governance.

Political leaders must prioritize integrity in their decision-making processes. This entails making choices guided by ethical principles, the rule of law, and the public's best interests.

When making policy decisions, leaders should set aside personal or party interests and focus on the greater good. Upholding integrity fosters trust among the public and ensures that political ambitions do not undermine the welfare of citizens.

Political leaders must be accountable to the public for their actions, policies, and promises. This includes transparency in decision-making, open communication, and responsiveness to public concerns.

Leaders should embrace mechanisms for public feedback, engage in meaningful dialogue, and actively address grievances. Being accountable can align political ambitions with the public's welfare.

Political leaders should ensure that their actions, including the allocation of resources, appointment of officials, and implementation of policies, are transparent and open to public scrutiny. Transparency prevents corruption, nepotism, and favoritism and ensures that political ambitions are pursued within the boundaries of ethical conduct.

Ethical governance requires the inclusion of diverse perspectives and meaningful participation of citizens in decision-making processes. Political leaders should foster an environment where all voices are heard, and decisions reflect the prerequisites and aspirations of the entire population.

By incorporating diverse viewpoints, leaders can ensure that their political ambitions are aligned with the welfare of marginalized neighborhoods and vulnerable groups. Conflicts of interest can arise when political leaders prioritize personal or party interests over public welfare. Ethical governance demands leaders identify and disclose potential conflicts and take appropriate measures to mitigate them.

This may involve recusal from decision-making processes or establishing independent oversight bodies to prevent undue influence. Leaders must demonstrate a commitment to serving the public interest rather than using their position for personal gain.

Political ambitions often come to the fore during election campaigns. Political leaders must uphold ethical standards in their campaigning practices. They should refrain from engaging in misinformation, spreading hate speech, or resorting to unethical tactics to gain an advantage. Fair and transparent electoral processes and ethical campaigning ensure that public welfare remains the primary focus in pursuing political ambitions.

Political leaders must consider the long-term implications of their decisions and policies. While short-term political gains may be appealing, they should not come at the expense of long-term sustainability. Ethical leaders consider their actions' social, economic, and environmental impacts, aiming to leave a pleasing and enduring legacy for future generations.

Recommendations

Balancing political ambition and public welfare is no small feat, but ethical governance requires it. Here are some recommendations:

- **Transparency:** Politicians should be transparent about the potential benefits and drawbacks of any pre-election social schemes.

- **Responsibility**: There should be mechanisms to hold politicians accountable for their promises and commitments.
- **Public Participation:** Ensuring public involvement in decision-making can add a layer of ethical scrutiny.
- **Long-term Planning**: Political leaders should focus on the long-term implications of their policies beyond just the next election cycle.
- **Ethical Audits**: An ethical audit of policies can provide an unbiased assessment of whether a scheme aligns more with public welfare or political ambition.

The ethical considerations surrounding political decisions are complex and multi-faceted. While political ambitions are a reality that cannot be ignored, they must be balanced carefully with the overarching duty toward public welfare. This requires ethical awareness and the courage to make decisions that may be politically risky but are in the public's best interest. The ultimate moral obligation of any politician should be to serve as a steward for the betterment of society, both in the immediate future and for years to come.

The intricate relationship between political ambitions and public welfare creates an ethical maze that is difficult to navigate. Political leaders must act as competitors in the political arena and stewards of the general interest, which often entails making morally complex decisions.

Ethical frameworks like consequentialism, deontological ethics, and virtue ethics can offer valuable perspectives but cannot eliminate the inherent challenges of political life. It remains essential for politicians to strive for a balanced approach, being transparent, accountable, and willing to engage with the public in addressing these ethical dilemmas. While political ambitions are a reality, they should not overshadow the ultimate moral obligation & must ensure the long-term welfare of the people.

Chapter Eleven

Media and Civil Society: Their Role in Scrutinizing Pre-Election Social Schemes

As per a report published in the UNESCO Digital Library in 2019, Credible elections require space for the exchange of competing perspectives and the often-robust contest for votes. Stakeholders must also inform, educate, and persuade the public to exercise their right to vote—or be voted for—without manipulation, intimidation, and violence. The spread of information pollution has become a critical challenge in elections, undermining trust in democratic processes, electoral management bodies, politicians, and the media.

Technology has revolutionized how candidates, electoral stakeholders, and voters interact and engage with one another. It can open pathways for political inclusion by providing virtual platforms of expression and information for often overlooked or unrepresented groups such as women or youth. Opposition parties have greater access to information about voters and the electoral process.

However, in recent years, the optimism about the potential of social media to reinvigorate public engagement in elections has given way to an increased alarm about the risks that a largely unregulated information sphere poses to electoral integrity.

The importance of independent traditional media in elections remains a core consideration, especially in countries where television and radio are valued sources of information. State-owned and public media need to be better funded and, therefore, more susceptible to government and other pressure to skew electoral coverage.

This is especially true of political reporting, which can be seen as a high-risk undertaking in volatile contexts due to threats of harm and malicious legal action directed against journalists and media outlets.

Harassment, attacks, and killings of journalists and subsequent impunity for these crimes have increased over the past several years and are particularly problematic during elections.

Programmatic Considerations

The need for more pre-emptive and longer-term interventions

Attempts to counter malign practices in the information environment around elections should be deployed earlier. Those intending to influence elections often begin those efforts months in advance and well before most election funding streams are accessible. It is also increasingly evident that electoral information pollution begins after the commencement of an election period, and it ends at the announcement of results.

Effective Convening and Partnerships

Strengthening electoral processes by recognizing and responding to malicious information operations that threaten the smooth running of elections requires a diverse range of organizations working together to form effective partnerships and collaborations.

Risks of over-reliance on digital and online solutions

The rise of digital tools and online election strategies is not without reason. They offer a low-cost way to enhance strategic communication, data analytics, voter engagement, media monitoring, and other critical tasks.

Learning and evaluation

Information integrity in elections is an evolving space for research and programming. Understanding the complex dynamics at play requires further investigation. Practical, programmable actions to address election-related information pollution are scattered and have yet to benefit from a robust learning agenda. Developing interventions to promote information integrity in elections with more robust evaluation methods of this programming needs to be undertaken to encourage innovation, cross-fertilization, and improved program design.

Let's understand this in detail.

Pre-election social schemes to garner public support can significantly impact the electoral landscape. While these schemes hold the potential to uplift discouraged societies and address socio-economic challenges, they also raise concerns about transparency, accountability, and political motivations. In this context, the role of media and civil society becomes crucial in scrutinizing pre-election social schemes.

The Role of the Media

The media plays an essential role in scrutinizing pre-election social schemes. Journalists can investigate the feasibility of these schemes, the cost of implementation, and the potential impact on the public purse. They can also hold politicians accountable for their promises and ensure they are not making false or misleading claims.

In a democracy, the media should be free and independent. This means they should be able to report on social schemes without fear of government interference. It also means that they should be able to hold politicians to account without fear of reprisal.

The Role of Civil Society

Civil society is another essential factor in scrutinizing pre-election social schemes. Civil society organizations, such as non-governmental organizations (NGOs) and think tanks, can provide independent analysis of these schemes. They can also raise awareness of these schemes' potential risks and benefits and help to ensure that the voices of the most vulnerable are heard.

Civil society organizations should be free to operate without government interference. They should also have access to the information they need to conduct their analysis. The critical role that media and civil society jointly play in the functioning of any democratic system cannot be overstated. These two pillars act as the checks and balances to governmental power, ensuring transparency, promoting political education, and voicing public concerns—one of the most intriguing aspects of their influence surfaces in the lead-up to elections.

The pre-election period often witnesses the implementation of various social schemes by the incumbent government, aimed ostensibly at improving the well-being of citizens but often critiqued as political ploys to win favor.

Media: The Fourth Pillar of Democracy

Often dubbed the "fourth estate," media shapes public opinion and sets political discourse agendas. Its power to influence comes from its mass reach and ability to frame issues. During the pre-election period, the media intensifies its scrutiny of government actions, particularly social schemes that might be aimed at appeasing specific voter demographics.

Let's understand the significance of broadcasting and civil society in ensuring transparency, promoting accountability, and safeguarding the integrity of such schemes.

The media acts as a watchdog, holding governments and politicians accountable for their actions. In the case of pre-election social schemes, the media's role is multi-faceted:

Information Dissemination

Information dissemination is a powerful tool that shapes societies and empowers individuals. It is pivotal in facilitating knowledge-sharing, promoting openness, and driving social progress. However, navigating vast information and combating misinformation requires critical thinking, media literacy, and collaborative efforts to ensure influential and responsible dissemination.

Effective information dissemination has a profound impact on various aspects of society. It enables individuals to make informed decisions, promotes democratic participation, encourages civic engagement, and holds institutions accountable. Education empowers students with knowledge, facilitating learning and intellectual growth.

In healthcare, it improves awareness, helps prevent diseases, and promotes healthy behaviors. It allows companies to communicate with customers, enhance brand reputation, and drive innovation. Information dissemination also contributes to social change by raising awareness about social issues, mobilizing communities, and facilitating collective action.

While information dissemination has numerous benefits, it also faces challenges. The sheer volume of information available and the prevalence of misinformation and disinformation make it difficult for individuals to navigate and access accurate and reliable information.

Language barriers, limited access to technology, information overload, and censorship can also hinder effective dissemination. Ensuring the credibility and accuracy of circulated information is also a significant challenge in an era where fake news and manipulated content can spread rapidly.

Media outlets are responsible for informing the public about the details, objectives, and implementation of pre-election social schemes.

They play a critical role in disseminating accurate and comprehensive information to ensure citizens are well-informed and can critically evaluate the impact and intentions behind these schemes.

Investigative Journalism

Journalists have the power to investigate and uncover potential irregularities, corruption, or misuse of resources in pre-election social schemes. Investigative reporting can bring hidden agendas, conflicts of interest, or exclusionary practices to light, ensuring transparency and accountability in implementing these schemes. Investigative journalism goes beyond surface-level reporting and delves deep into uncovering hidden truths, exposing wrongdoing, and holding those in power accountable. In an era of rapid information flow, investigative journalism is crucial in maintaining transparency, promoting social justice, and safeguarding democracy. It serves as a watchdog, serving the public interest by scrutinizing institutions, uncovering corruption, and revealing information that would otherwise remain hidden.

It is critical in ensuring transparency, accountability, and good governance. By digging deeper into stories, investigative journalists challenge the status quo and expose social injustices, corporate malpractice, government corruption, and human rights abuses.

Investigative journalism requires persistence, meticulous research, data analysis, and confidential sources and often involves working on long-term projects. Investigative journalists employ various methods such as document analysis, interviews, undercover operations, and data-driven investigations. However, investigative journalism faces numerous challenges, including threats to press freedom, legal and financial constraints, risks to personal safety, and difficulty accessing sensitive information.

Moreover, powerful entities may attempt to undermine or discredit investigative journalists' work, leading to reputational risks and potential backlash.

Let's explore more in this area

- **Fact-Checking and Verification:** Media organizations can fact-check claims made by political leaders and verify the effectiveness, reach, and impact of pre-election social schemes. This ensures the public receives accurate information, reducing the risk of misinformation or manipulation.

- **Public Discourse and Analysis:** Media platforms provide space for public discourse, analysis, and debate on the merits and drawbacks of pre-election social schemes. By presenting diverse perspectives, media outlets facilitate informed discussions that contribute to a more comprehensive understanding of the schemes' implications. It involves the examination and evaluation of information, evidence, and arguments systematically and objectively.

The analysis enables individuals to identify biases, logical fallacies, and inconsistencies in discourse, fostering a more nuanced understanding of complex issues. It helps individuals develop critical thinking skills, question assumptions, and make informed judgments.

Opinion Shaping: Editorials, opinion pieces, and televised debates can shape how the public perceives these schemes. By offering space for experts, activists, and average citizens to voice their opinions, the media helps generate a balanced view. The public can decide whether the scheme is genuinely beneficial or merely an electoral gimmick.

Through analysis, individuals can distinguish between reliable and unreliable information, recognize underlying power dynamics, and navigate the complexities of public debates. Public discourse and research are integral to the functioning of a democratic society. They foster the exchange of ideas, promote critical thinking, and empower individuals to make informed decisions.

By engaging in thoughtful analysis and participating in public discourse, citizens contribute to the vitality of democratic processes and the betterment of society.

Civil Society: The Collective Conscience

Civil society, comprising non-governmental organizations, community-based groups, and activists, plays a vital role in advocating for public welfare and scrutinizing pre-election social schemes. Civil society organizations (CSOs) can independently monitor and evaluate the implementation of pre-election social procedures. Through on-the-ground assessments, data collection, and citizen feedback mechanisms, CSOs can furnish insights into the schemes' effectiveness, identify gaps, and suggest improvements.

Civil society acts as a bridge between the government and the citizens, ensuring that the voices and concerns of the affected assemblies are heard. CSOs can facilitate community engagement, empowering individuals to actively participate in decision-making processes and hold authorities accountable for implementing pre-election social schemes.

It can advocate for transparency and accountability in designing, implementing, and evaluating pre-election social schemes. They can explore establishing independent oversight mechanisms, support the adoption of clear eligibility criteria, and advocate for public access to information related to the projects.

Civil society is vital in analyzing the legal and policy frameworks that govern pre-election social schemes. CSOs can examine the compatibility of these schemes with constitutional provisions, human rights standards, and international best practices. Civil society can contribute to improving and refining these schemes through legal advocacy and policy recommendations.

There is a significant role of media and civil society in scrutinizing pre-election social schemes, which becomes more effective when they collaborate and synergize their efforts. Let's understand them one by one.

- **Information Sharing and ground-level monitoring:** Media organizations can collaborate with civil society groups to access information, expertise, and ground-level insights. This collaboration enhances the accuracy and depth of reporting, providing a more holistic understanding of the schemes' impact. Organizations can monitor the on-ground implementation of these schemes, using empirical data to gauge their effectiveness. They can also serve as whistle-blowers if they find discrepancies in the distribution of benefits, thus ensuring a more equitable system.

- **Public Awareness Campaigns:** Communication channel outlets and civil society organizations can jointly undertake public awareness campaigns to educate citizens about their rights, entitlements, and the potential implications of pre-election social schemes. These campaigns can empower individuals to question and evaluate the procedures, fostering a sense of informed citizenship.

- **Advocacy for Reforms:** Platforms can amplify the voices of civil society organizations advocating for reforms in pre-election social schemes. Through investigative reports, interviews, and opinion pieces, outlets can generate public support for necessary policy changes and improvements in these schemes.

- **Peer Accountability:** Media organizations and civil society groups can hold each other accountable for their respective roles. Civil society can monitor coverage for accuracy and impartiality. In contrast, the media can scrutinize civil society organizations for transparency and ethical conduct. This peer accountability ensures a robust and thorough scrutiny process.

- **Policy Analysis:** Civil society frequently dissects government policies, drawing from an interdisciplinary approach that combines economics, social science, and political theory. Often published as white papers or reports, these analyses serve as valuable resources for the media and the public.

Civil society and other modes of expression are indispensable in scrutinizing pre-election social schemes, ensuring transparency, accountability, and public welfare. Civil society organizations contribute to informed decision-making and public awareness through investigative journalism, fact-checking, community engagement, monitoring, and legal analysis.

While both these entities operate independently, their work often complements each other. Media outlets may pick up reports and findings from civil society organizations, thus giving them a platform for broader visibility. Conversely, civil society often relies on media reports for initial leads into issues that warrant further investigation. In a well-functioning democracy, this symbiosis is essential for effectively scrutinizing pre-election schemes.

Case Studies

In countries like India, pre-election schemes like subsidized food grains or free electricity have often been a point of public debate. Media and civil society played pivotal roles in these debates, employing a mix of investigative journalism and empirical analysis to examine these schemes' actual impact. In the United States, debates around social programs like Obamacare witnessed intense scrutiny from media outlets and civil society groups, providing the electorate with diverse perspectives.

Challenges and Ethical Considerations

While the roles played by media and civil society are laudable, they come with challenges. The increasing trend of sensationalism in media and the threat of "fake news" can distort facts. Civil society organizations are not entirely immune to political influences and may have their agendas. Ethical journalism and unbiased research are paramount in maintaining credibility.

The media and civil society serve as the gatekeepers of democracy, particularly in the volatile pre-election period. Their rigorous scrutiny of social schemes ensures that governments are held accountable for their actions and prevents the propagation of policies that are purely electoral in their intent. Despite the challenges posed by internal and external pressures, these institutions continue to uphold democratic integrity through fact-based reporting, analytical depth, and public engagement. As long as these pillars stand firm, the roots of democracy will delve deeper, making it more resilient against the whims of transient political gains.

By upholding their roles as guardians of public interest, the media, or multiple communication channels, civil societies can contribute to the practical and equitable deployment of pre-election social schemes, promoting the well-being of citizens and the integrity of democratic processes.

While the landscape is fraught with challenges, ranging from media bias to shrinking civic spaces, the importance of these institutions still needs to be recognized. Through cooperative efforts, the media and civil society can act as robust checks against the possible manipulation of social schemes for electoral gain, thus safeguarding the integrity of the democratic process.

Safe, fair, and credible elections continue to face new and emerging challenges from information pollution. Tools available to malicious actors intent on disrupting the information ecosystem around elections continue to develop apace, and responses to counter these threats require ongoing, multisectoral collaboration.

Chapter Twelve

Lessons from International Experiences: Comparative Analysis

While India has implemented several successful social schemes, and there is no doubt about it, valuable lessons can be learned from countries with successful social welfare programs.

Let's explore some of these countries and the key lessons that can be drawn from their experiences to enhance their social schemes' design, implementation, and impact.

1. Nordic Countries: Denmark, Finland, Norway, Sweden

The Nordic countries are renowned for their comprehensive social welfare systems. Critical lessons for our country include:

- **Universalism**: Nordic countries prioritize universal social schemes, ensuring all citizens can access essential services and benefits. Our country can learn from this approach and consider implementing universal social schemes to ensure inclusivity and reduce administrative complexities.

- **Strong Social Safety Nets:** Nordic countries have well-developed social safety nets that yield financial support and social protection to vulnerable populations. We can focus on strengthening its social safety net programs to ensure no one is left behind.

- **Holistic Approach:** Nordic countries adopt a holistic

approach to social welfare, emphasizing not only income redistribution but also investing in quality education, healthcare, and childcare facilities. We can adopt a similar approach, addressing multiple dimensions of well-being to ensure unceasing and comprehensive social development.

2. Brazil: Bolsa Família Program

Brazil's Bolsa Família program is one of the most extensive conditional cash transfer programs globally. Critical lessons for us include:

- **Targeted Approach:** Bolsa Família effectively targets the poorest and most vulnerable populations through a well-defined identification process. India can enhance its targeting mechanisms to reach those in need more accurately.

- **Conditional Cash Transfers:** Bolsa Família combines financial assistance with conditionalities, such as school enrolment and healthcare utilization. India can consider introducing similar conditionalities to assist human capital elaboration and ensure a long-term impact of social schemes.

- **Integrated Service Delivery:** Bolsa Família facilitates coordination between various government departments, enabling integrated service delivery. India can focus on improving interdepartmental coordination to enhance comprehensive guarantees to beneficiaries.

3. South Africa: Social Grants System

South Africa's social grants system provides financial assistance to vulnerable groups, including children, older people, and people with disabilities. Critical lessons for us include:

- **Simplified Application Process:** South Africa has simplified the application process for social grants, making it more accessible and reducing administrative burden. We can streamline its application procedures to ensure ease of access for beneficiaries.

- **Electronic Payment Systems:** South Africa has successfully implemented electronic payment systems for social grants, reducing leakages and ensuring efficient and transparent fund disbursal. We can leverage technology to enhance payment systems and minimize corruption.

- **Regular Evaluation and Adjustments:** South Africa continuously evaluates its social grants system and adjusts based on changing socio-economic conditions. We can prioritize regular monitoring and evaluation to ensure the effectiveness and relevance of its social schemes.

4. Singapore: Central Provident Fund (CPF) System

Singapore's Central Provident Fund (CPF) system is a mandatory savings scheme that provides citizens with retirement, healthcare, and housing benefits. Critical lessons for us include:

- **Long-term Savings:** The CPF system promotes long-term savings and individual responsibility for retirement and healthcare expenses. We can emphasize the importance of personal savings and financial planning as part of its social schemes.

- **Multi-Purpose Fund:** The CPF system serves multiple purposes, including retirement, healthcare, and housing. We can explore integrating various social welfare components into a cohesive framework to maximize efficiency and impact.

- **Mandatory Contributions:** Singapore's CPF system is based on mandatory employee and employer contributions. We can consider implementing similar compulsory contribution schemes to ensure sustainability and broaden the resource base for social projects.

5. The National Health Service (NHS) in the United Kingdom

This program provides universal healthcare to all UK citizens, regardless of income or employment status. The NHS is one of the most popular and successful social schemes globally.

Learnings from the schemes mentioned above are:

- **The importance of targeting:** Many of the most successful social schemes target their benefits to specific groups, such as people experiencing poverty, older people, or people with disabilities. This helps ensure that the scheme's benefits reach those who need them most.

- **The importance of coordination:** Many social schemes are more effective when coordinated with other government programs. This helps ensure that people stay caught up and get the help they need.

- **The importance of monitoring and evaluation:** Monitoring and evaluating social schemes to ensure they are effective and reach their intended beneficiaries is essential. This information can be used to improve the systems and make them more effective in the future.

Learning from countries with effective social schemes can share valuable insights to enhance their own social welfare programs' design, implementation, and impact.

The Nordic countries' emphasis on universalism, Brazil's targeted, conditional cash transfer approach, South Africa's streamlined application processes and regular evaluation, and Singapore's focus on individual responsibility and multi-purpose funds all offer valuable lessons. By incorporating these lessons, India can improve its social schemes, ensuring inclusivity, transparency, efficiency, and long-term sustainability for the betterment of its citizens' lives.

Chapter Thirteen

Rising Population: A Serious Challenge for Social Schemes

The world's population is expected to reach 9.7 billion by 2050, up from 7.9 billion today. This rapid population growth will put a strain on resources and social schemes around the world.

One of the biggest challenges posed by a rising population is the increasing demand for food, water, and energy. As the population grows, so too will the need for these resources. This could lead to shortages and higher prices, which could have a negative impact on the poor and vulnerable.

Another challenge a rising population poses is the increasing demand for healthcare and education. As the population ages, more people will need access to healthcare services. There will also be more children who need to be educated. This could put a strain on healthcare and education systems, which could lead to lower-quality services.

A rising population threatens social schemes such as pensions, unemployment benefits, and social security. As the population ages, fewer people will work and pay taxes to support these schemes. This could lead to cuts in benefits or even collapse some strategies altogether.

India, the world's second-most populous country, faces an unprecedented challenge in managing its soaring numbers. The population is estimated to be over 1.4 billion and continues to grow.

While a large population can offer advantages such as a vast labor force and diverse talent pool, it also presents unique challenges, particularly in the domain of social welfare. The rising population significantly impacts the effectiveness and reach of social schemes, creating a complex issue for the government.

Despite having the best intentions, the Indian government grapples with the reality of effectively providing and implementing social schemes for such an expansive populace.

Let's understand some challenges due to the rising population.

Strain on Resources

A continually growing population puts immense pressure on finite resources. Government schemes aiming to provide food, education, healthcare, and other basic amenities must grapple with ever-increasing demand. This often leads to either dilution of benefits or the unfortunate exclusion of deserving beneficiaries. Even when schemes are well-intentioned, the sheer numbers can make effective implementation extremely challenging.

Fiscal Constraints

The funding required for large-scale social schemes increases proportionally with population growth. Managing the fiscal deficit while adequately funding these initiatives is a tightrope walk for any government. With an increasing number of people to support, the financial burden becomes unsustainable in the long run, impacting other sectors like infrastructure development and defense.

Quality vs. Quantity

When the focus shifts to serving an expanding population, the quality of services often takes a backseat. For instance, the government might successfully create more hospitals and schools in healthcare and education, but the standard of care and education may decline. The challenges of scale inhibit the ability to provide high-quality, impactful services.

Administrative Overheads

A significant population necessitates an enormous administrative apparatus to implement social schemes effectively. The logistics of reaching millions of people, particularly in rural and remote areas, can be overwhelming. Inefficiencies, corruption, and mismanagement often creep into the system, affecting the optimal utilization of resources.

Targeting and Inclusion Errors

Given the vast and diverse population, accurately identifying the beneficiaries of any social scheme becomes an exceedingly complex task. Errors of both exclusion (needy people left out) and inclusion (undeserving people included) are more likely to occur when dealing with larger population sizes. Such errors compromise the effectiveness of social programs and dilute their intended impact.

Gender Bias

Another dimension that complicates the implementation of social schemes in the face of a rising population is gender. Many methods inherently suffer from gender biases or do not adequately address the unique needs of women. Given that women comprise almost half of India's massive population, any shortcomings in this area are magnified, further straining social welfare objectives.

Policy and Political Implications-Short-Term vs. Long-Term Goals

The rising population often pushes governments towards short-term measures aimed at immediate relief rather than long-term sustainability. This tendency is particularly pronounced during elections, when new schemes or sops may be announced to garner votes. These short-term schemes often lack the structural integrity to provide long-lasting solutions, leaving the population in a perpetual state of dependency.

Here are some specific actions that can be taken to address the challenges of a rising population:

Invest in family planning programs.

Family planning programs can help couples plan their families and reduce the number of births. This is one of the most effective ways to slow population growth.

- **Public-Private Partnerships:** Engaging the private sector can bring in additional funding and expertise in management and technology. Such partnerships can be designed to address specific challenges posed by a rising population, creating more sustainable and effective social welfare programs.

- **Promote Sustainable Development:** Sustainable development is the development that meets the needs of the present without compromising the ability of future generations to meet their own needs. This means using resources efficiently and equitably and protecting the environment.

- **Reform Social Schemes:** Social schemes such as pensions, unemployment benefits, and social security must be reformed to make them more sustainable and equitable. This means ensuring that these schemes are adequately funded and that they reach the people who need them most.

Technological Interventions

One avenue for making social schemes more practical despite the rising population is leveraging technology. Digital databases, real-time monitoring, and automation can substantially reduce administrative overheads and improve targeting accuracy. The Aadhaar biometric identification system is one such example that aims to minimize fraud and streamline service delivery.

Invest in education and healthcare.

Education and healthcare can help people improve their lives and reduce poverty. This is also important for ensuring that everyone has the opportunity to reach their full potential.

Regional Disparities

India is a diverse nation with varying population densities and socio-economic conditions across its states. Some states are more populous than others, leading to uneven distribution of social benefits. As resources are stretched thin, these regional disparities can deepen, causing social and economic imbalances.

India's rising population presents a dual challenge to effectively implementing social schemes. Not only does the sheer volume of beneficiaries put a strain on resources, but the associated complexities of administration, identification, and governance make the task even more daunting.

It exacerbates the difficulties in planning, funding, and executing social schemes. Although the challenges are daunting, they are not insurmountable. Solutions may involve innovative public-private partnerships, the use of technology for better targeting and delivery, and revisiting the scale and scope of schemes to align them with demographic realities. Nonetheless, the task remains herculean, demanding concerted efforts from all stakeholders to ensure that social schemes can achieve their intended goals in a society marked by such vast numbers.

Chapter Fourteen

The Competitive Environment of Pre-Election Social Schemes in Indian States: A Double-Edged Sword

India's vibrant democracy and diverse political landscape are a matter of pride and complexity. The country's federal structure allows individual states considerable autonomy in governance, including the launch of social schemes for welfare and development.

One notable aspect of electioneering is the promise of social schemes, frequently introduced just before elections to woo voters. While this trend is global, it is particularly prominent in India, where political parties often promise an array of social welfare programs.

As elections approach, there is often a flurry of such social plans introduced by various states, ostensibly for the benefit of citizens. However, this phenomenon also leads to an intriguing yet under-discussed scenario—a competitive environment not just between rival political parties but within the state governments themselves.

Globally, pre-election social schemes are not uncommon. The United States has seen this with tax cuts and relief packages, while the UK has occasionally introduced social benefits and National Health Service (NHS) reforms before elections. However, what sets India apart is the scale and diversity of these schemes.

This is due to several factors, including the rise of regional parties, the increasing importance of social media, and the growing awareness of voters about their rights. Regional parties have played a significant role in the growth of pre-election social schemes. These parties often have a solid support base in particular regions, and they can target their plans to these voters.

Contextualizing the Competition

In a democracy as complex as India's, elections are not limited to the national arena. Often staggered across years, state elections create a perpetually 'electoral' atmosphere. This setting induces states to launch social schemes targeting specific voter groups, from subsidizing farming equipment to offering free laptops for students.

The competition arises when one state's innovative scheme gains nationwide attention, prompting other states to release similar or improved versions. At first glance, this is a win-win situation for citizens who reap the benefits. However, a closer examination reveals several nuances that need to be considered.

The competitive environment for social schemes in India is fierce for the following reasons.

- **Political Plurality:** With multiple national and regional parties competing, each seeks to outdo the other in promises. There is a growing body of research that suggests that there is a link between the competitive environment and political plurality. Studies have shown that countries with more competitive markets tend to have more political parties and more inclusive political systems.

Political plurality refers to the existence of a variety of different political parties and interest groups. It is often seen as necessary for a healthy democracy, as it allows for the peaceful coexistence of different viewpoints and the representation of all segments of society.

- **Diverse Demographics:** The diversity of India means that schemes must cater to various cultural, linguistic, and many more. In India, one size only fits some. What works for the

Punjabi farmer may need to be more effective for the IT professional in Bengaluru. A scheme aimed at empowering women in urban settings could miss the mark entirely when transplanted to a rural backdrop. Hence, any policy or initiative must be sensitive to its target demographics' cultural ethos and practical realities.

- **Media Scrutiny:** The extensive media coverage means any promise made is dissected, debated, and could become a double-edged sword. On the one hand, comprehensive media coverage can amplify the reach of a social scheme, providing free publicity and winning over voters. A well-planned, socially beneficial proposal can earn a politician goodwill, propelling their chances of electoral victory. If the media coverage is favorable and the proposed scheme addresses genuine societal concerns—such as unemployment, healthcare, or education—the politician's message can resonate far beyond their immediate constituency.

However, the same media spotlight that can elevate a good plan can dissect and eviscerate a poorly conceived one. Journalists will investigate the scheme's feasibility, financial experts will comment on its economic viability, and social activists will scrutinize its inclusivity and ethics. The media's analysis can be devastating if a proposal appears to be an impractical, empty promise designed solely for political gain.

The Global Context

The competitive environment for pre-election social schemes is familiar to India. It is a problem in many countries around the world. For example, in the United States, both the Democratic and Republican parties have promised to expand social welfare programs in the run-up to elections.

The reasons for this competitive environment are complex. One reason is that voters increasingly demand more government intervention in the economy. Another reason is that the media has made it easier for voters to compare the promises of different parties. Finally, the rise of social media has made it easier for parties to target their contracts to specific groups of voters.

Let's check the global trends below.

- **Mature Democracies:** In established democracies like the US or the UK, the trend leans towards less radical, more sustainable promises, often because of a stringent policy review process. When a new policy proposal emerges, it is subject to intense scrutiny from various stakeholders, including legislators, think tanks, media, and the public. This scrutiny often begins even before a bill reaches the floor for debate. Experts in relevant fields analyze the proposed policy, its financial viability, its impact on various social groups, and its legal implications. Bills may undergo multiple revisions and negotiations before they become law, making the entire process slow but deliberate.

- **Emerging Economies:** Like India, countries like Brazil and Nigeria also witness a surge of pre-election promises focusing on social welfare. Contracts range from subsidized housing, better healthcare facilities, free education, and direct cash transfers. Such commitments, while not unique to emerging economies, take on heightened significance given the broader aspirations of these nations to uplift millions from poverty and integrate them into the mainstream economy. However, the success of these promises often depends on the robustness of the underlying administrative infrastructure and the genuine intent of politicians.

- **Authoritarian Regimes:** In non-democratic countries, social schemes are often announced to give the semblance of a fair election process. In such nations where authoritarian regimes hold sway, elections if held at all, often lack the elements that characterize a genuinely democratic process. Such governments, however, are not oblivious to the power of public perception—both domestically and internationally. They frequently announce grand social schemes during elections to create an illusion of fairness and responsiveness to citizen needs.

The Concept of Good, Bad, and Ugly

The Good

- **Benchmarking:** A competitive environment encourages states to benchmark their schemes against those in other states, often resulting in more robust and innovative programs.

- **Issue Highlighting:** Popular schemes focus on neglected issues, making them nationally significant.

- **Democratization of Benefits:** When multiple states offer similar schemes, more people benefit regardless of geographical location.

The Bad

- **Short-Termism:** In the race to outdo each other, state governments may prioritize quick wins over long-term sustainability.

- **Financial Unsoundness:** The lure of electoral gains can sometimes push states into launching financially unsustainable schemes, leaving future administrations to handle the burden.

- **Duplication of Efforts:** Multiple states implementing similar schemes without sufficient customization can lead to resource wastage.

The Ugly

- **Populism Over Pragmatism:** The temptation to lure voters with grand promises can often result in poorly thought-out schemes that serve more as election propaganda than genuine welfare programs.

- **Erosion of Trust:** Citizens may become cynical about the genuine intent behind these schemes, affecting the electoral prospects and the social contract between citizens and their government.

Lessons

Several instances demonstrate this competitive dynamic among Indian states. For example, introducing a particular scheme in one of the eastern parts of India aimed at aiding small farmers and sharecroppers prompted other states to revise their existing strategies or introduce new ones focusing on agrarian welfare. While it drove attention to the struggles of small farmers, it also led to hastily implemented programs in some states with questionable long-term viability.

Similarly, the competitive launch of educational schemes, often involving the free distribution of laptops or tablets to students, has mixed results. While they have significantly improved access to digital learning, they have also raised questions about the state's ability to provide after-sales service, maintenance, and, more crucially, quality educational content.

Implications for Governance and Democracy

- **Accountability:** A competitive environment can lead to better accountability as governments strive to outperform each other.

- **Policy Convergence:** The risk of policy convergence without sufficient localization is high. One size does not fit all, especially in a country as diverse as India.

- **Citizen Engagement:** The active role of citizens in demanding accountability and transparency becomes even more critical in such a context.

The Way Forward

There are several ways to address the problems caused by the competitive environment for pre-election social schemes. One way is to reform the electoral system. For example, a proportional representation system would make it more difficult for any party to win a majority of seats, reducing the incentive for parties to make unrealistic promises.

Another way to address the problem is to improve transparency and accountability. This would make it more difficult for parties to engage in corruption. Finally, educating voters about the actual costs of social schemes is essential. This would help voters to make informed choices when they vote.

The competitive environment for pre-election social schemes is a complex problem with no easy solutions. However, it is essential to address this problem, as it can have a few negative consequences for the economy and democracy. By reforming the electoral system, improving transparency and accountability, and educating voters, we can help to create a more sustainable and equitable environment for social schemes.

In addition to the above, here are some other things that can be done to address the problems caused by the competitive environment for pre-election social schemes:

- Strengthen the oversight of social projects by independent bodies.

- Make it easier for people to access information about the actual costs of social strategies.
- Promote public debate about the role of social schemes in society.

By taking these steps, we can ensure that social schemes promote the common good rather than serve the narrow interests of political parties.

The phenomenon of competitive social schemes among Indian states, triggered by the approach of elections, offers a fascinating lens to evaluate the complexities of governance in a federal structure. While competition can catalyze innovation and improvement, it also brings with it the risks of financial imprudence, short-termism, and an erosion of public trust.

For this competition to enrich Indian democracy, states must balance electoral expediency with financial prudence and long-term vision, keeping the true welfare of the citizens at the forefront.

Chapter Fifteen

Strengthening Governance and Ensuring Sustainable Social Welfare Policies

In contemporary society, governance and social welfare policies are closely intertwined. While governance sets the structural framework for decision-making and policy implementation, social welfare policies exemplify the state's role in delivering social justice, economic stability, and overall well-being. The essence of governance goes beyond mere politics or administration; it involves an inclusive mechanism that coordinates resources, institutions, and societal actors to achieve collective goals.

It involves an inclusive mechanism coordinating resources, institutions, and societal actors to achieve collective goals. Likewise, sustainable social welfare policies go beyond short-term relief measures; they aim to create lasting social equality and economic mobility frameworks.

To begin with, governance necessitates transparency, accountability, and civic participation.

Transparency allows for information sharing, making public processes easily understandable and accessible. It enables public scrutiny, thereby reducing the chances of corruption or inefficiency.

Accountability holds actors—governmental bodies, private sectors, or individuals—responsible for their actions. For governance to be effective, it must provide mechanisms through which aggrieved parties can claim redress, thereby maintaining a system of checks and balances.

Civic participation ensures that governance is not a top-down process. Through community engagement, citizens can voice their needs, opinions, and concerns, making governance more responsive and adaptive to the complexities of societal needs.

Effective governance sets a fertile ground for the germination of sustainable social welfare policies. Traditional welfare policies often focus on immediate needs, offering temporary relief but seldom resolving underlying systemic issues. The concept of sustainability calls for long-term solutions that address root causes, not just symptoms. This implies designing policies with a life-cycle perspective, considering the impacts on future generations and current populations.

A well-governed system would utilize data-driven research methods for policy formulation. Policymakers can create more targeted welfare programs using scientific evidence, expert consultations, and demographic studies. These programs range from universal healthcare, quality education, and employment opportunities to mental health services, housing solutions, and environmental protection. A comprehensive welfare system that covers these multiple aspects enhances the quality of life and reduces social and economic inequalities.

Another dimension to consider is the financial sustainability of social welfare policies. Good intentions are not enough; the welfare system must be economically viable to be sustainable. This involves sound fiscal policies, balanced budgets, and prudent resource allocation. Effective governance will thus incorporate risk assessments, future projections, and contingency plans to ensure that welfare policies can adapt to unforeseen circumstances such as economic downturns or natural disasters.

Given the rapid changes in technology, economy, and

demographics, static policies are more likely to become obsolete or ineffective; therefore, social welfare policies should also be flexible and adaptive. Strong governance structures allow for regular reviews, amendments, and improvements in policy frameworks. It involves a continuous process of evaluation based on performance metrics and public feedback.

Moreover, governance and social welfare cannot operate in isolation; they must be integrated into the broader regional and global context. With globalization, issues like migration, climate change, and international trade require cooperative governance mechanisms and harmonized welfare policies. A sustainable approach would be to align national policies with global agendas like the United Nations' Sustainable Development Goals, which aim to tackle global challenges through collaborative efforts.

Strengthening governance is not merely a technical or bureaucratic endeavor but an ethical obligation. It demands an unwavering commitment to social justice, equity, and human dignity. Similarly, sustainable social welfare policies are not mere financial or logistical arrangements but embody a society's values, aspirations, and sense of responsibility towards its citizens. When governance is robust and accountable and social welfare policies are comprehensive and sustainable, they create a virtuous cycle, enhancing each other and contributing to a more just, equitable, and resilient society.

When governments are effective, transparent, and accountable, they are better They are also better able to protect the rights of the most vulnerable, such as women, children, and older people.

Likewise, sustainable social welfare policies go beyond short-term relief measures; they aim to create lasting social equality and economic mobility frameworks. Therefore, strengthening governance and ensuring sustainable social welfare policies are imperative for a just, equitable, and resilient society.

India is a vast and diverse country with a population of over 1.3

billion people. The government has made significant economic and social development progress in recent decades. However, significant challenges, including poverty, inequality, and corruption, still need to be addressed.

Strengthening governance and ensuring feasible social welfare policies are critical for achieving an unbiased outcome in India. Effective governance mechanisms and justified policies play a crucial role in addressing socioeconomic disparities, promoting social justice, and improving the quality of life for all citizens.

Good governance is essential for ensuring that the country's resources are used effectively and efficiently and that the merits of buildout are shared equitably. Good management is also necessary for promoting transparency and accountability and for protecting the rights of citizens.

For India, ensuring that the country's resources are used effectively and efficiently and that the ease of enhancement is shared equitably is essential.

Another critical challenge facing India is ensuring unceasing social welfare policies.

To strengthen governance and ensure continual social welfare policies, India must prioritize the following:

- **Access to Information:** Enhancing citizens' access to information related to social welfare policies, including their design, implementation, and evaluation, fosters transparency and empowers individuals to hold policymakers accountable.

- **Open Data and Disclosure:** Promoting the proactive disclosure of information, such as budget allocations, expenditure details, and outcomes, allows for public scrutiny and accountability.

- **Whistle-blower Protection:** Establishing robust mechanisms to protect whistle-blowers who expose corruption, malpractice, or misuse of resources within social welfare programs ensures accountability and discourages wrongdoing.

An important area, i.e., active citizen participation, is crucial for all-embracing social welfare policies.

India can strengthen citizen engagement through the following:

- **Public Consultations:** Conduct regular public consultations during the formulation and review of social welfare policies to gather diverse perspectives, insights, and feedback from affected communities.

- **Grievance Redressal Mechanisms:** Establishing accessible and responsive grievance redressal mechanisms that enable citizens to voice concerns, seek resolutions, and hold authorities accountable for addressing issues within social welfare programs.

- **Civil Society Collaboration:** Partnering with civil society organizations to harness their expertise, leverage their community networks, and ensure the inclusion of disadvantaged groups in policy formulation.

Beyond this, coherence among social welfare policies is crucial to ensure effectiveness, avoid duplication, and maximize resource allocation.

India can enhance policy coherence by:

- **Integration and Coordination:** Promoting coordination and collaboration among different ministries, departments, and levels of government to avoid fragmentation and ensure a holistic approach to social welfare policies.

- **Intersectoral Collaboration:** Encouraging collaboration between social welfare programs and sectors such as health, education, employment, and housing to address multidimensional challenges vulnerable populations face.

- **Impact Assessment:** Conduct regular impact assessments to evaluate the interlinkages and effectiveness of various social welfare policies, identify synergies, and make necessary adjustments to achieve desired outcomes.

The time has come to build a robust institutional capacity essential for constructive governance and viable social welfare policies. We are enhancing government officials' skills, knowledge, and capabilities for designing, implementing, and monitoring social welfare programs to ensure efficient service delivery.

They are spreading decentralized governance structures that empower local authorities, enabling them to tailor social welfare policies to the specific work of their networks and ensure effectual implementation.

We are establishing rigorous performance evaluation mechanisms to assess the efficiency, effectiveness, and impact of institutions responsible for social welfare policies, encouraging accountability and continuous improvement.

Social welfare policies are essential for providing a safety net for the poor and vulnerable and endorsing social inclusion. Social welfare policies can help to reduce poverty, improve health and education, and publicize gender equality. Feasible social welfare policies require adequate and tenable resource mobilization.

India can explore various avenues for resource mobilization:

- **Broadening the Tax Base:** Implementing progressive tax reforms ensures that the burden of funding social welfare programs is shared equitably among different income groups.

- **Public-Private Partnerships:** Engaging the private sector through public-private partnerships to leverage additional resources, expertise, and innovation to enact social welfare programs.

- **International Cooperation:** Exploring partnerships with international organizations and multiple agencies to access additional funding, technical assistance, and best practices in social welfare policies.

Strengthening governance and ensuring admissible social welfare policies are essential for India's future. A few other factors could affect the success of efforts to strengthen governance and ensure reasonable social welfare policies in India. These factors include:

- The political will to implement reforms.
- The level of public backup for reform.
- The capacity of government institutions to implement reforms.
- The availability of financial resources.

The success of these efforts will depend on the ability of the government to address these challenges and build a strong foundation for well-grounded development.

In an increasingly interconnected world, the accomplishment of successful social schemes requires international cooperation and knowledge sharing.

Governments, policymakers, and social welfare organizations can benefit greatly from learning from each other's experiences, best practices, and innovative approaches to address complex socioeconomic challenges.

Challenges and Way Forward

- **Political Will:** Without political commitment, governance reforms and sustainable social policies will remain on the back burner.

- **Resource Constraints:** Limited resources necessitate prioritization, which can be contentious.

- **Public Awareness and Education:** Public engagement is crucial for demanding better governance and more sustainable policies.

- **Innovation and Adaptability:** As societal needs change, governance structures and social welfare policies must evolve.

Strengthening governance and ensuring the sustainability of social welfare policies are intertwined objectives that demand a comprehensive, multi-pronged approach. Good governance is not just an administrative requirement but a fundamental right that can enhance the effectiveness and sustainability of social welfare policies.

Financial prudence, environmental consideration, and socio-cultural sensitivity should be integrated into policy design and governance structures.

In conclusion, governance and sustainable social welfare policies are interconnected domains that significantly influence a nation's well-being. Strengthening governance through transparency, accountability, and civic participation lays the groundwork for sustainable, effective, and responsive social welfare policies. By focusing on long-term solutions and integrating these policies into the broader regional and global context, we can ensure they are economically viable, socially equitable, and ethically sound. We can build a more just, honest, and sustainable future through holistic, integrated approaches.

References

- The Times of India
- Vikaspedia
- Orrissa Post
- Organisation for Economic Co-operation and Development
- Myschemes.gov.in
- Economic Times
- RBI Bulletin June 2022. 115. State Finances: A Risk Analysis
- Nagrika
- Unesco Digital Library; Social media & Election 2019; Promoting information integrity in elections.

About the Author

Praveen Rao is a visionary technology leader and esteemed public sector expert. With a keen understanding of the intersection between technology and governance, Praveen has become a driving force behind digital transformation initiatives that have revolutionized the public sector landscape.

Fascinated by the power of innovation to shape society, He pursued a degree in Personal Management from the University of Pune, A Diploma in Business Management from SBS, Pune, Public Health Management from Yale University, and leadership Management from the Indian School of Business, Hyderabad.

Praveen Rao and his wife Akanksha Rao founded Capturing Life Foundation, a Non-Profit Organization that works around digital literacy.

Capturing Life Foundation actively promotes Social Media Awareness programs, Fake Content exposure & many other social activities.

His foundation understands the far-reaching consequences of misinformation and the potential harm it can cause to individuals and society at large. Through collaborations with experts in media literacy, fact-checking organizations, and digital security specialists, the foundation actively works to expose and debunk fake content, providing individuals with the tools to analyze information and make informed judgments critically.

His deep technical expertise and his unwavering commitment to public service set the stage for his remarkable career as a technology leader in the public sector.

Praveen has consistently sought to harness technology's potential to improve citizens' lives and enhance government operations. He has spearheaded groundbreaking initiatives that have modernized outdated systems, streamlined processes, and increased transparency in public institutions. His ability to navigate complex bureaucratic landscapes and collaborate with diverse stakeholders has made him a trusted advisor to government officials and a sought-after speaker at prestigious conferences.

He regularly publishes articles and delivers thought-provoking keynotes on the future of technology in the public sector. His forward-thinking insights and innovative ideas continue to shape the discourse around digital transformation and its impact on governance.

With his profound knowledge, unwavering commitment, and transformative vision, Praveen Rao is a true pioneer in leveraging technology for the betterment of society. His exceptional leadership and expertise have positioned him as a guiding light in the public sector, inspiring others to embrace the possibilities of technology and drive positive change in the world.

*To know more about Praveen Rao
and his work, please visit.*

www.praveenrao.in

www.capturinglifefoundation.in

We love creating beautiful books for you!

Come be a part of our ever-growing community of authors. Grow, write, and publish with us!

Scan here to explore books, authors and more

Connect with us on socials. We'd love to hear from you!

    Inkfeathers Publishing